POSTMODERN
PUBLIC
ADMINISTRATION

POSTMODERN PUBLIC ADMINISTRATION

TOWARD DISCOURSE

CHARLES J. FOX
HUGH T. MILLER

SAGE Publications
International Educational and Professional Publisher
Thousand Oaks   London   New Delhi

For information address:

SAGE Publications, Inc.
2455 Teller Road
Thousand Oaks, California 91320

SAGE Publications Ltd.
6 Bonhill Street
London EC2A 4PU
United Kingdom

SAGE Publications India Pvt. Ltd.
M-32 Market
Greater Kailash I
New Delhi 110 048 India

Printed in the United States of America

Library of Congress Cataloging-in-Publication Data

Main entry under title:

Fox, Charles J.
    Postmodern public administration : toward discourse / Charles J.
Fox, Hugh T. Miller.
        p. cm.
    Includes bibliographical references and indexes.
    ISBN 0-8039-5801-3. (cl).—ISBN 0-8039-5802-1 (pb)
    1. Public administration. 2. Postmodernism—Political aspects.
3. Policy sciences. 4. Constructivism (Philosophy). 5. Critical
theory. 6. Discourse analysis. I. Miller, Hugh T. (Hugh
Theodore). 1953-   . II. Title.
JF1411.F67 1995
350—dc20   94-32843

95 96 97 98 99 10 9 8 7 6 5 4 3 2 1

Sage Production Editor: Diana E. Axelsen

Contents

Foreword

This book irritates many corners of my brain and psyche. It fails to support several of my cherished norms about public administration. Some of its philosophical distinctions remind me of the tendentious theological disputation of the Middle Ages. I lose patience with the authors' thickness of withering critique on the one hand and thinness of practical proposals on the other. Among the targets of devastating critique is the work of my Blacksburg colleagues, no less. I have every reason to hate the book. Yet I love it! Why?

Because it typifies what is best about our field of the study of public administration at this time in its development. Our top current teaching, scholarship, theorizing, and consulting—even if untidily based in competing paradigms, incommensurate epistemologies, and rival worldviews—is *vital.* No matter whether you agree with it or not, find it useful or not, or consider it an advance or a deterioration, you must agree that public administration's current intellectual life is animated, feisty, energetic, lively, and loudly argued.

And so is this book. Fox and Miller describe themselves as "late-blooming working-class kids." As such, they take on the world of public administration theory with gusto and fearless determination. In one sweep, they reject perhaps 90% of accepted public management doctrine as an orthodoxy that is intellectually bankrupt and democratically unacceptable. Then, in another sweep, they brush aside what they see as the leading competitors to the orthodoxy, constitutionalism (their label, not mine) and communitarianism. Next, without missing a beat, they rush headlong into constructing a new theoretical position they call constructivism, based on critical theory, phenomenology, and structuration theory. From this intellectual platform they then build a "discourse" theory of public administration. Our old friend and enemy bureaucracy, meanwhile, is replaced by a marvelous synergistic image, "public energy fields."

More boldness is difficult to imagine. Each time I went over the book in manuscript form my motors raced. Our field is now more than a century old and goodness knows we *need* excitement; well, here's some! Yet the audacity of Fox and Miller has a second value: Their review of the doctrines and philosophies they crucify or resurrect is itself informative. Seldom have I seen the epistomological-ontological issues of the field laid out so starkly. One is jarred awake by the journey and educated at the same time. The reader receives a kind of intellectual train ride, at about the speed of a Japanese *shinkansen,* from the Enlightenment's assumptions about human cognition up through modernism's reification of metanarratives and postmodernism's neotribal hyperreality. The scenery along the way is described in a dramatic, concise, pithy, even punchy prose, something like we used to find on the good sports pages of newspapers around the country. Brace yourself when you turn to Chapter 1.

Another way in which the book typifies the best in current public administration thinking is its idealism. I am using that word not in its formal philosophical sense, of course, but to denote an underlying dedication to such norms as *true* democracy and *true* community. Fox and Miller champion open rather than restricted access to public policy making; they display a healthy populist contempt for "brass-nameplate" institutions; and they call for instituting public policy dialogue that is authentic, sincere, honest, and genuine. How more old-fashioned can your values get?

This deep-seated interest in, and dedication to, the fundamental moral principles of a democratic, egalitarian, and free polity is, however, nothing radical or unusual for our field. Public administration has always evinced a moral content. Whereas most academic disciplines glorify objectivity, neutrality, and aloofness from the messiness of the world, our studies and teachings have never done this. We have always been concerned about the condition of the world, from our Progressivist beginnings and mid-century outpourings against totalitarianism through the new public administration and contemporary debates over gender and ethnic diversity, the empowerment of citizens, the meaning of public interest, bottom-up planning, and a host of other themes. Even though Fox and Miller militantly eschew most of the field's theoretical superstructure, they are curiously "traditional" in the sense of carrying on with this habit of worrying about not only what's true and what's false, but what's right and what's wrong.

As you move through these exciting pages you will discover a disgust, even contempt for foundationalism, that is, any notion of "canonical" or absolutist universality. There is no final right or wrong, in other words. This notion, which incidentally is preeminently axiomatic to the very postmodernists our authors are so anxious to transcend, leads them to denounce both the normative musings of my Blacksburg colleagues and the citizen participation dogmatism of communitarians. Both schools of thought base themselves, it is alleged, on reified symbolizations of structures embedded in the controlling metanarratives—a sanctification of the constitutional founding in the one case and an elitist abstraction of community in the other. The only advantage the constitutionalists have over the communitarians, we are told, is that whereas the latter are scattered across the country, the former all live in Blacksburg and can thus construct a more complete argument.

Those of us at Virginia Tech will be glad to accept any compliments we can get! I shall do so on behalf of my colleagues but not defend here the merits of our position, whatever they may be. This is not the place to explain our Manifesto or discuss the place of the Constitution in American public administration. I shall, however, use the privilege given me as introducer of this fine book simply to comment that I do not think anyone needs to apologize for articulating a normative underpinning for the U.S. public sector, whether or not it fits the latest "sophisticated" theories of knowing and being. Moreover, I do not think anyone needs to feel belittled or dominated if one's belief system happens to coincide with those of other citizens. Among my public values are free speech, honest elections, and lawful authority, despite any dangers that I have thereby succumbed to ruling metanarratives. Perhaps nationhood or brotherhood as a transcendent intersubjective reality is not, after all, a bad way to live together in the world.

In short, whether intellectually derived or simply felt in the pit of your stomach, purposeful believing is a part of being human. The canonical universality of that feeling is less important than how it is internally compelling as we go about the daily tasks of living or administering. Whether our belief systems as private individuals or public administrators are "true" is less important than that they are *ours*.

Fox and Miller actually end up taking this kind of relativist position themselves, via habituated reality construction under Giddens's structuration theory. If asked, I am sure they will admit that their own belief systems stem too from constructed reality systems. Indeed, our authors work harder than most of us in doing the construction. The overall point I am making is that the values that seem to shape their vision of ideal public administration are darn good, even if not eternally valid.

Fox and Miller are not only "right" in this sense, they want to propose something useful. This is another reason I am so attracted to their work. Unlike many of our fashionable critics of modernism—that is, the deconstructionists and postmodernists—Fox and Miller do not simply play "French Intellectual." That is to say, they do more than spend the entire afternoon sipping cappuccino on the boulevards, desponding darkly over the irreversible deterioration of the human condition. Our authors are, to the contrary, almost embarrassingly upbeat. They see themselves as developing a new discourse theory of public administration that will be a constructive and positive step for democratic public administration and for the quality of public policy. As they put it in one of their eloquent turns of phrase, they aspire to midwifery, not funeral directing. Here again, our authors typify the best of public administration discourse. Their book is not only exciting and informative, it demands that we raise our moral sights and do something active about improving the works of humankind.

Indeed, I sincerely hope that this book will not be just a stimulating theoretical essay that will be dutifully read by doctoral students and no one else. My own feeling is that improved discourse along the lines they advocate could be a significant step in the right direction, if appropriately buttressed by an infrastructure of some good brass-nameplated institutions. At the same time, the democratic "feedback loop" they see as so fraudulent will not easily disappear, and in my view should not do so. Discourse must operate within the context of publicly agreed-upon rules of the game and leadership selection—regardless of their faults—or the whole polity will fall apart. Moreover, as Fox and Miller admit, their discursive ideal will not by itself deliver public services. The public energy field will have to do some mundane work, such as plowing the city streets in winter and policing the public parks in the summer. At best, its two proponents agree, the new discursive ideal will lie in the background rather than forefront of the practitioner's daily acts.

Their concern for practical application is not without wisdom, for the world of public administration theory has of late had a tendency to enter a world of discourse of its own, isolated from policy and practice. Increasingly the theorists and the practitioners talk about different subjects in different venues and languages. Fox and Miller remind us that the history of civilization is full of abstract thought that races beyond everyday life. Let us not allow that to happen in our realm of public collective action—which is, after all, of, by, and for the citizenry; here, irrelevance is not a harmless curiosity but a subtraction from focused effort in the public weal.

Enough of my scattered impressions and reactions. It is time for you, the reader, to get on this intellectual bullet train and form your own impressions and reactions. I hope you enjoy the trip as much as I. By actively listening to Fox and Miller on their own terms, and by reacting honestly with your own thoughts and words, you will have contributed to the kind of discourse our authors brilliantly propose.

Charles T. Goodsell
Virginia Polytechnic Institute and State University

Preface

We seek to redirect thinking about public policy and administration in light of the postmodern condition. We will hold that this condition can, in the realm of governance, be ameliorated by successive approximations toward authentic discourse. This is no mere incremental adjustment. It requires bold steps away from well-worn paths. Many cherished presuppositions will be debunked. We do not expect all readers to be pleased. And, in the spirit of discourse, we reserve the right to agree with those who disagree with our formulations.

In the pages that follow, we argue that American representative democracy is neither representative nor democratic. Sovereign will formation is not happening. Lacking sovereign legitimacy, top-down bureaucratic rule is but petty autocracy. Worse, the postmodern condition that we describe deprives the culture at large of any robust basis in shared reality from which the sovereignty of the whole people might be reasserted. Increasingly we traffic in symbols without experiential referents.

To the extent that these speculations are valid, all proposals to fix the machine of governance are fruitless. The raw materials it once processed are depleted, no spare parts are available, and the company that produced it went bankrupt in the mid-50s. Nostalgia for it only delays the need to ask each other: What should we do next?

In light of this analysis of governance in postmodernity, we make a normative process proposal. Let's move away from hierarchical bureaucracy. No legitimate democratic input energizes it from the top. Let's move toward discourse, an inherently democratic structure of will formation. Now, moving away from bureaucracy is no simple matter. We see our task as theorizing its transcendence. This requires, in turn, a kit bag of conceptual tools, some borrowed, some reforged for the task at hand. We call the kit bag constructivism. The tools are engineered to break down that aging rusted machine and the institutional parts of which it is composed. Once "bureaucracy" and "institutions" are understood as reified, that is to say, once we recognize that contingent human practices are mistakenly objectified as immutable forces of nature, then the hard boundaries—between and among agencies, institutions, and bureaucracy, and these distinguished from the citizenry—can be made permeable. Instead of looking at policy and administration processes as a series of power transactions between walled institutions, we propose instead an energy field conceptualization. A public energy field is composed of a multiplicity of malleable democratic discursive social formations. In this way we seek to affirm current nascent discourse formations such as policy networks, interagency task forces and consortia, negotiated regulatory constraints, adhocracies and the like. Under "warrants for discourse," we propose a model (based on Habermasian ideal speech discourse) by which such formations may be judged as democratic, tending toward democratic, or likely false starts.

An unfortunate side effect of theorizing outside the banks of the mainstream is the need to employ concepts and the language by which they are known, which may be unfamiliar to our mind's-eye readers, public administrationists. Indeed, many of the concepts and much of the language we use at first will seem foreign to the literature into which we wish this book to be insinuated. Many of the concepts we use are appropriated from current philosophy, and although we have aspired to concise, tight, and meticulous progression of exposition, reading this book may require reader effort. We want to thank you in advance for that effort; we hope it will be worth your while. We have tried to be entertaining. Overall, though, we are deadly serious. As Mr. Dooley might say, "Postmodern politics ain't beanbag."

A number of others in the field of public administration, we hasten to note, have been exploring many of these same themes. The thinkers who have enlivened the discussions at the annual Public Administration Theory meetings are most deserving of our gratitude. Indeed, this work was forged in that crucible of authentic discourse. In addition, we appreciate the work of Michael Harmon, the first to develop a fully articulated theory for proactive public administration; Sam Overman, who readily recognized chaos theory as a deterministic project and showed us a better physics metaphor, namely quantum theory; Dwight Waldo, who enunciated orthodoxy's perdurability most clearly; Gary Wamsley, whose work on policy subsystems in the face of "iron triangle" prejudices has helped us understand the vitality of discourse participation, and to bring a referent to our discourse theory. Others who have influenced in various ways the shape of this book include Guy Adams, Mary Timney Bailey, Bayard Catron, Clarke Cochran, Rick Green, Barry Hammond, Ralph Hummel, Budd Kass, Harvey Kaye, Larry Luton, Frank Marini, Steve Ott, Michael Parenti, Denny Snook, Cam Stivers, and Dvora Yanow. Charles Goodsell deserves special thanks, and not only for writing the foreword. Speak with him at any length and you will know that he has mastered substantially more than the field of public administration— and in that field he is a hero. He is an astute observer of civic space, and more than that, a gracious listener. To follow Professor Goodsell around for a couple of days is to learn a great deal about decency.

We would like to do the clever little thing that authors do in prefaces, and claim that despite the best efforts of peers we nonetheless persist in our errors and we take full responsibility. But alas, this would not be true. The above mentioned, and many we neglect, have always said "go for it." So we did.

This book is dedicated to Chuck's son, Harold Fox, and Hugh's mother, Evelyn Miller.

Charles J. Fox
Hugh T. Miller

PART ONE

Critique

1 A New Approach to Democratic Governance

As an acceptable model of governance, orthodoxy is dead. Orthodoxy (Waldo, 1948) was that enduring prescription of neutral public administration ascribed to Wilson (separation of politics and administration), Taylor (scientific management), and Weber (hierarchical control). Orthodoxy, at its high point in the decades surrounding World War II, was a manifestation of the period that recent philosophers have identified as *high modernism.* We are referring to that 25-year period when the industrial economy matured and the ideology of technocracy and electoral-style procedural democracy prevailed in culture and politics, a period sometimes called "the American Century." This was before the Vietnam War became bad news.

Since then, orthodoxy has died a thousand deaths, by a thousand cuts. The ever-apparent discretion exercised by administrators in policy formulation— not only implementation—makes a mockery of the Wilsonian dichotomy. Taylorism has been savaged by at least three generations of human relations social psychologists. The effort to sublimate political conflict into technical-rational domains was only sometimes successful. Strict chain-of-command hierarchy (never more than an ideal type for Weber) has been challenged by contemporary developments in Japanese management, by the TQM (total quality management) movement, by the "reinventing government" tendency, and in the move to devolve authority so as to involve employees in decision making.

Despite its death and regardless of the eager academic pallbearers, the spirit of orthodoxy hovers over the study of public administration, insinuating itself in all theories of governance and in every actual public agency. Orthodoxy now has the status of legitimizing myth. It is the background assumption of all mainstream reform efforts. The inertial force of orthodoxy

3

is its legitimacy, but this legitimacy derives from a nostalgia that craves certainty and structure. The residues of orthodoxy shape the modules and sequencing of academic curricula and such personnel practices as civil service reform and performance appraisals. Reform efforts to date seek not to go beyond orthodoxy, but to resuscitate it.

Uniquely, the field of public administration is poised between, on one side, the theoretical endeavors of political science, philosophy, economics, organization theory, sociology, and social psychology, and, on the other, the daily practice of governance. Public administration scholarship is well-positioned to bury orthodoxy and propose alternatives to it. Because academic public administrationists find themselves between praxis and theory—we have been charged to educate the governors—we have direct knowledge of the maladies of orthodoxy. We have paradigm anxiety, and paradigm anxiety foments creative theoretical endeavor.

In the field of public administration, two alternative models today contend to displace orthodoxy: (a) constitutionalism or neoinstitutionalism and (b) communitarianism or civism. We seek in this book to bring forth a third, discourse theory. This book, then, ambitiously attempts both to affirm with other nascent clusters (not yet full-fledged schools of thought) the demise of orthodoxy, and then also to show why constitutionalism and communitarianism are not as satisfying as the discourse theory we offer. To briefly foreshadow our argument, they are both concerned with legitimizing public administration. Constitutionalists ask: What—aside from legislative statute—justifies what we do? Communitarians are concerned with legitimizing a new sovereign, not the legislature but the citizens themselves. They ask: How—aside from legislative statute—can we justify what we do? We, on the other hand, are less concerned with legitimacy and more concerned with policy. We write against the backdrop of this more important question: What should we do next?

The Argument

A. ORTHODOXY AND ITS ALTERNATIVES

Our thesis contains many arguable elements that challenge mainstream assumptions. The theorizing that we produce is eventually optimistic, but we begin skeptically. The *representative democratic accountability feedback loop* model of democracy, we claim, does not work in any way that can be called democratic. The procedural democracy theory—which begins with individual preferences that are aggregated to popular will, codified by legislation, implemented by the bureaucracy, and evaluated in turn by attentive voters—lacks credibility. This *loop model* not only lacks credibility as a whole process, but also none of its stages function as orthodox theory supposes they do. The politics side of the infamous politics-administration dichotomy does not work systematically in service to democracy. The corollary attempt to realize the popular sovereignty by precisely enunciating rules to bind the behavior of governmental functionaries is misguided because of the dysfunctions of the loop. It is also undemocratic at the worksite level. Furthermore, the exponential articulation of rules cannot bind administration. The more rules that are promulgated, the more must an administrator *choose* a particular concatenation of them.

Although many of the maladies of orthodoxy emanate from the loop, reform efforts nonetheless assume the validity of the loop and instead scapegoat the bureaucracy. In a classic bait and switch move, malfeasance and neglect of duty by elected officials (in the Watergate scandal, for example) resulted in the symbolic corrective of ethics reform and civil service reform. The legislation that was enacted at an ethical turning point, the post-Watergate era, was nothing more than the imposition of a whole new layer of regulatory rules on the career bureaucracy, ineffective, of course, in preventing the subsequent Iran-Contra scandal or the Keating Five savings and loan scandal. Ethics reform served to reinforce the loop model. We were repeatedly reminded that "the system works" when, instead, the loop should have been further discredited by these scandals. Similarly, failures in the political system were visited on the administrative personnel system by imposing measures such as performance appraisal to bring the bureaucracy under control of the politicians whose own malfeasance brought about the legitimacy crisis to which civil service reform was offered as corrective. The maladies of loop democracy are then exacerbated again with the scapegoating of career civil servants beginning in the 1970s and reaching a crescendo in the 1980s.

This discordant tone evoked academic defense of proactive administration, like that found in the Blacksburg manifesto. This elaborate constitutional argument was an attempt to show that nonelected public servants owe allegiance first to the Constitution and only secondarily to the current incumbents of elected and politically appointed office. This argument was a well-intentioned life buoy thrown to drowning bureaucrats and a refreshing, innovative alternative to the loop orthodoxy. Despite its virtues, the Blacksburg manifesto fell short of meeting the need for an alternative model for public administration. Neither the elected inhabitants of the loop nor the public, which has sullenly acquiesced to their rule, will be convinced by arcane constitutional scholarship. It is a weak attempt to legitimize the administrative state. The strategy entails accepting the bureau-pathologies associated with traditional, progressivist public administration. We judge it to be too conservative to serve as the template for governance in the postmodern period.

The maladies of loop democracy also brought forth a communitarian alternative, which interrupts the loop by directly accessing citizens. Citizen activation, civism, and similar tendencies in public administration literature represent a serious contender to replace the orthodox model. The major strength of these efforts is that they are the manifestations in public administration of philosophical communitarianism, a view of politics which possesses a fully articulated ontology, epistemology, and cosmology rooted in ancient, medieval, and postmodern thought. Democracy, to communitarians, is not a mere procedural arrangement of dispute resolution. Citizens need to be involved in the decisions that affect their lives because it is an important aspect of communitarian teleology, of being fully human. But the communitarian ideal is too remote from current conditions to be workable. The authors of this book are communitarians in the sense of embracing many aspects of the communitarian ideal. We nonetheless assert the need for a discourse theory, in part because of our assessment of postmodern conditions wherein the communitarian ideal is unlikely to be realized. The problem is not merely that civic participation consumes too many evenings and weekends or that citizens possess "false consciousness"—although these are part of the difficulty. "The community" may not be attentive enough to solve either your public problems or ours.

B. POSTMODERN PROBLEMATIC

We are concerned in this book with political discourse; the public policy conversation that has been eclipsed by glib, insincere, attention-grabbing symbolic imagery. And we tend to this matter with the help of postmodern thought. Postmodern thought has conceptualized theoretically some of the nagging problems of public awareness that we believe have affected the health of the body politic. Postmodernists have developed the best vocabulary we know of to understand this aspect of public life. Accommodate yourself to their terms, we will urge, because the mundane language of modernity won't work. Tendencies in the larger culture and society—gathered up under the terms *postmodernism* and *postmodernity*—should be taken into account in attempts to replace orthodoxy. Particularly salient is what we call the thinning of "reality" or the development of *hyperreality*. This term is used to indicate that signs and words have become increasingly estranged from more authentic communities of discourse.

Most of what passes for public conversation is not that at all. It degenerated as communication lost the check on authenticity provided by dialogue. Outrageous claims—that light beer "tastes great," for example—stand unchallenged, because the media of discourse are monologic. Also notable is the fatuous triviality of this and other claims offered in the public conversation. Worse, in conditions of hyperreality, words lose their capacity to signify and instead become *self-referential,* that is, meaningful only in a narrow context that is either not shared by everyone or fleeting in the sense that there is nothing beyond the moment to digest. In the beer commercial, the "debate" is prefigured, and we are left to contemplate whether light beer is (a) less filling or (b) tastes great. Because the message is self-referential, obvious options that reside outside the self-referential (and monologic) discourse are not presented: (c) it bloats the stomach and (d) it tastes awful. With this sort of monologic banality dominating the media, the macroculture—which is nationwide and crosses generational, class, race, linguistic, and gender divisions—thins. Thicker, more robust, communities of discourse do develop, but only in enclaves or subcultures (a tendency referred to as *neotribalism*).

These two dialectically related tendencies—thinning macroculture and robust subcultures—make democratic will formation and policy discourse increasingly problematic. This leads, in turn, to a simulated politics wherein political entrepreneurs traffic in abstract political symbols rather than deeds. Thus simulated politics restrains substantive policy making. Whether by design or accident, such development is profoundly conservative, favoring those who benefit from the status quo. The fragmentation and neotribalism of postmodern consciousness—already focused on the hyperreal media images—make governance of any kind difficult. Hence postmodern conditions will (a) further strain the already tenuous connection between the orthodox loop model and democratic ideals; (b) make constitutionalism an unlikely legitimation ploy; and (c) hinder the development of civic community, a precondition for communitarian governance.

So we seek a new framework that can withstand postmodern conditions, on the one hand, and can claim congruence with democratic ideals, on the other. We start from the ground up. We select our theoretical underpinnings carefully to avoid the many postmodern traps that we have identified.

C. THEORETICAL GROUNDING FOR DISCOURSE THEORY

Theoretical presuppositions condition how things are perceived. For example, command-and-control bureaucracy would be nonsensical without the kindred assumptions of cause-and-effect determinism and rational utility-maximizing individuals. These underlying premises and assumptions shape understandings, the propositions that stem from those understandings, and the possibilities for action that may then be imagined. We find that the underlying assumptions endemic to most public administration theorizing have led to the ongoing intellectual crisis, now decades old, a crisis that is even more poignant in postmodern conditions.

Mostly, too much is assumed by prevailing ontologies—too much is assumed about the rationality of human nature, about the concreteness of organizations and institutions, about the consensus around organizational goals, and about the solidity of the key concepts and variables that shape public administration thought. We try to back away from as many of these assumptions as possible, and even go so far as to allow that "reality" itself is neither concrete nor objective, but constructed by humans and hence malleable.[1] In the process of backing away from these underlying assumptions, we come to understand that many of the categories that we uncritically employ in daily discourse are *reifications,* that is, socially constructed categories that are mistaken for things that exist "out there" in the world of "objective reality." Reified categories are those that are unsuitably endowed (by their human creators) with autonomous, nonhuman force and are thought to exist independently of human social interaction.

Bureaucracy is a case in point. We often speak of "organizational goals" as if these goals were somehow separate from the goals of specific groups of humans and therefore should be privileged. Public agencies, private corporations, and bureaucratic organizations of all stripes are thought to "behave," to possess desires, and to have wants and needs just like us people. The courts have gone so far as to give corporations rights of free speech, as if they were citizens! What sense can be made of these invisible institutional structures that somehow seem real? Anthony Giddens's structuration theory is of great help here. He grounds institutions in social processes, a conceptualization that allows us to avoid reifying institutions, but also allows us to appreciate that there are social-structural constraints on our possibilities for action. Bureaucracy, Giddens teaches, is a structuration of repeatable practices, a conglomeration of habits, patterns of social practices that recur in rule-like fashion. Bureaucracies are but social habits and social constructions, or to use Giddens's term, *recursive practices.* This perspective on organizations—that they are social constructions rather than concrete entities—is derived also from Peter L. Berger and Thomas Luckmann's (1966) *Social Construction of Reality,* which serves as a useful reminder that we humans actively participate in creating the categories that prefigure our knowledge of the world. To avoid reifying socially constructed categories, we shed assumption after assumption until we arrive, with Maurice Merleau-Ponty as our guide, at the precategorical lifeworld.

We will explain the salient features of Merleau-Ponty's phenomenology later, but two notions might be immediately useful in this introductory overview. The first is the notion of *the situation.* When we pay attention, we must pay attention . . . to something. There is always a situation whenever our attention is called forth. When we solve a problem, we solve a specific problem, located in a specific situation within a particular context. If we can ground our deliberations in a situation, we can arrest the postmodern tendency toward detached symbolic hyperreality that designates no actual situation as referent. A situation reconnects our symbols to terra firma. The second concept that Merleau-Ponty teaches is the notion of *intentionality.* In confronting a situation, we are seldom content to observe passively; we may want to take action. Perception is for action. We bring intentionality to the situation, and situations are loaded with possibilities for actualizing or foiling intentions. Intentionality is a useful concept because it prepares us for public policy discourse, where participants are concerned not only to understand the situation, but to take action with respect to it.

Then, with the help of quantum physics, we learn to break from our atomistic entities: the rational individual and the bureaucratic organization. Physicists studying quantum mechanics were able to surmount the constraining influence of the atomic particle, and we public administrationists likewise can open a new line of theory.

Our ontological foundation laying takes a radical turn. We boldly assert that bureaucracy should no longer be the dominant theme in the study of public administration. We seek a new way of looking at public administration, premised on an indeterminate collection of phenomenological moments we call a *public energy field.*

We revive Kurt Lewin's field theory at this point and update it with a phenomenological twist. *Field* is the complex of forces that bear on the situation. The structure of the field follows no set formula, but depends on what is happening in the lifeworld. We demarcate for public policy only those fields that contain matters of public concern and possess vitality or energy.

The term *energy* implies that the field is sufficiently charged with meaning and intention that people are aroused, alert, and attentive.

Field contrasts markedly with *bureaucratic organization,* which is premised on the formula of hierarchical control. The preoccupation with structure implied by concepts such as bureaucracy and organization may be viewed as the cordoning off of irregular, perhaps tumultuous forces that are out there. Fully acknowledging the situation and its field of forces might be inopportune because, although these forces can sometimes be anticipated, they may not be controllable. Field does not structure its boundaries for purposes of control; rather, the situation (or the collection of relevant situations that may extend over space and time) brings its own set of constraints and opportunities.

The public energy field is the playing field of social discourse; here is where public policy gets created and re-created. Now if public policy is generated in an energy field of public discourse, and if we care about democracy, we are obligated to ponder: Is there any way of making this discourse democratic?

D. WARRANTS FOR DISCOURSE

Admission to the discourse ought to be free of charge. This openness stands in stark contrast to the status quo ante. Under the influence of the loop model, where policy is ratified by legislatures penetrable by monied special interests, it is likely that meanings will be captured and policy will be crafted on behalf of the wealthy, the well-organized, and the special interests that fund election campaigns and purchase media time and space. The powerful can ensure that certain classes of people are excluded from the debate, canceling their opportunity to offer a different interpretation of events. People are excluded from the debate for reasons having nothing to do with the merits of their claims. Among those so excluded are public administrators—under the norms of orthodoxy. Those with a genuine claim, including public administrators freed from institutional boundaries, ought to be able to argue that claim where it matters—in the public conversation. Public administrators freed from institutional boundaries are part of the people.

Because action, and not truth, is the ultimate effect of the deliberation, discourse is inherently political. As Deborah Stone pointed out, policy analysis is the art of strategically crafting persuasive arguments. This presentation of policy arguments takes place within the context of ongoing recursive practices—usually it is proposed that some social institution be altered, adjusted, or created anew. The struggle that ensues is a struggle for meaning captured in an environment in which no meanings are a priori true or ontologically fixed. Meaning is up for grabs.

With meaning up for grabs, the temptation to offer specious attestation is strong. A bit of misrepresentation just might get us what we want. But, like a virus, speciousness is infectious. Why bother attending a discourse where claims are as likely to be counterfeit as authentic? So we propose that certain forms of conduct should, figuratively speaking, get one removed from the playing field on the grounds that the possibility of popular will formation is doomed if the discourse is ruined for everyone. To preserve the discourse, the rest of us will take permission to *not listen* to claimants who offer inauthentic claims. Those claimants can lose their warrants.

We borrow from Jürgen Habermas's theory of ideal speech, communicative competence, and discursive redemption to craft a policy discourse that is democratic and authentic. Habermas's theory of authentic speech acts envisions speech that presumes sincerity of the speaker, clarity of expression, accuracy of what is claimed, and relevance of utterances to the context of the discussion. If any of these is brought into doubt, it is assumed that a speaker could discursively redeem them by explaining the deeper or higher principles justifying the authenticity of the speech acts (or, conversely, admitting it was just a joke and withdrawing the claim). We have taken this notion of communicative standards and have applied it to policy discourse.

We move beyond Habermas's model when we introduce Hannah Arendt's notion of agonistic tension. In the discourse we can expect a struggle over meanings; we expect argumentation, claiming, and counterclaiming, not harmonious consensus, as the participants try to resolve what to do next. But discipline is needed in such a discourse. We propose sincerity, situation-regarding intentionality, willing attention, and substantive contribution. These are the warrants for discourse.

Sincerity of the speaker means that arguments offered in the public forum are sincere, earnest, honest, and genuine. There are various methods of argumentation that lack these characteristics, and we describe several that we have adduced. Situation-regarding intentionality is the second warrant for discourse. This warrant assures that the discourse will be *about* something, about contextually situated activities. Speakers with situation-regarding intentionality will take into account the context of the problem, the lives of those affected, and the public interest. Third, speakers who are willingly attentive have been heeding the conversation as it has developed and offer their participation willingly (they are neither coerced nor are they apathetic). Finally, the substantive contribution warrant relieves the other participants from having to suffer free riders and fools. The forms that substantive contribution might take cannot be delineated in advance, but some of the usual ones are analytic and/or synthetic competence. Sharing of relevant experience derives from the standpoint of the situation whereas data analysis derives from the standpoint of expertise.

Everyone has a presumptive right to the discourse, and warrants are freely available. But human groups develop norms when they contemplate social action; hence implied warrants can be lost by those who violate the implied rules of the structuration. No, we do not intend to take away the free speech rights of those who wish to speak inauthentically. But we would refuse a request to take such claims seriously, as we do authentic claims. An authentic discourse, we believe, does not suffer liars, fools, charlatans, the self-indulgent, or the ethical egoist. What to do next is too important a question to be sullied by purposely inauthentic utterances.

We have laid out our discourse theory, and the next task is to demonstrate its veracity. Can evidence of public policy discourse, as we have articulated it, be found?

E. NASCENT FORMS OF DISCOURSE

Case material that purports to be democratically discursive is examined, and a typology stemming from warrants for discourse is advanced. The typology serves as a way of assessing claims that a method or example is democratic. We first establish a category of those cases whose discourse seems most like elite-dominated monologic manipulation (few-talk) and contrast this category against anarchistic expressionism (many-talk). Both prove unsatisfactory when held up to the standards of authentic discourse. However, many-talk that is sustained over time begins to develop structuration and coherence and may develop into approximations of the kind of authentic discourse we were hoping to find. We refer to this cast of discourse as some-talk.

Some-talk discourse describes those nascent structurations identified in the public policy literature as policy networks. The rules of authentic discourse are perceptibly in evidence in many public policy networks. Public administrators, policy experts from industry groups and public interest groups, legislators, and other kinds of citizens do try to make sense, together, of a situation. Further, they are trying to make sense of the situation as a prelude to action—there is an open question about what should be done next that energizes the participants and their interactions, creating momentum and the possibility of change.

Policy networks as such are not always ideal applications of the model—powerful participants are often able to exclude the less powerful; sometimes the motivating force is nothing but self-interest; many policy proposals are but self-aggrandizing ploys; the arguments offered are not necessarily sincere. But the discourse model provides a set of criteria against which the authenticity of a policy conversation can be judged. Our hope is to encourage those forums that are intimations of authentic discourse and expose as inauthentic those that are either monologic manipulations at one end of a continuum or those that are merely cathartic, anarchic babel at the other end. The findings are not always encouraging.

But we would not suggest the possibility of discursive democracy were there not real intimations of it. Institutionally and hierarchically transcendent networks of publicly interested discourse provide a feasible model for public administration. We find that some policy networks, interagency consortia, and community task forces exhibit potential for discourse. In these nascent forms, we find that experts, policy analysts, public administrators, interested citizens, process generalists, and others participate together to work out what to do next. There are occasions where meaningful, situation-regarding discourse occurs.

Authentic discourse is the best hope for a democratic theory of governance that takes into account postmodern conditions. Discourse theory is an accurate model in the sense that it describes events that can be observed and normative in the sense that it provides criteria for assessing authentic discourse. When compared to the communitarian ideal, discourse theory is a "weak" form of democracy, but unlike communitarians, we cannot be accused of forcing people to be free for their own good. We are not fully satisfied with discourse theory in that it does not entail those aspects of "strong democracy" embraced in communitarianism. Discourse theory envisions a democracy of all, but only those who embrace the *res publica* (public thing) will participate. All, including public administrators, who accept the responsibility of authentic participation represented by the warrants will strengthen democracy with their participation.

Note

1. Our habit of placing quotation marks around the word *reality* is designed to avoid the quagmire of ontological disputation. This is not the place to decide whether "reality" as we know it exists independently of the questions humans ask about our sensuous environment and the sense we communicate to each other through gestures and signs.

2 Orthodoxy and Its Alternatives

In the field of public administration, the demise of orthodoxy has called forth two alternative models: (a) neoinstitutionalism or constitutionalism and (b) communitarianism or civism. We seek in this book to bring forth a third, discourse theory. Now, all three alternative models may be considered discretionist (Fox & Cochran, 1990). That is to say, they affirm a proactive public administration on behalf of the public interest. Administrative discretion, in turn, is based explicitly or implicitly on the incredulity of representative democracy as we know it (called weak democracy by Adams, Bowerman, Dolbeare, & Stivers, 1990; known also as overhead democracy and unilateralism in Mosher, 1982). All discretionist views imply a disdain for contemporary political authority.[1] Although discretionists dismiss the politics/administration dichotomy, they also would like to leave behind the petty bickering, inauthentic grandstanding, and gridlock that stem from partisan politics. This preference may be affirmed by what this chapter first accomplishes: a brief rehearsal of what we call descriptively, if inelegantly, "the representative democratic accountability feedback loop" and its corollary, reliance on rules. Second, despite these manifest flaws in American governance, most calls for reform presuppose the efficacy of the loop model. Ethics regulations and civil service reform foisted upon career public servants illustrate the point. The best known alternative model, constitutionalism or neoinstitutionalism as developed in the Blacksburg manifesto, is the topic of the third section. This body of discretionist thought is congruent with the first two points and indeed is a reaction to the bureaucrat bashing associated with ethics and personnel reforms. If the loop fails to deliver sensible manifestations of popular will, administrators can turn to the Constitution for legitimacy and guidance. We conclude Section 3 by arguing that constitutionalism is an insufficiently radical departure from orthodoxy for it attempts constitutional legitimacy for the extant administrative state with all its flaws. More to our liking is, fourth, the communitarian tendency, which seeks to replace the loop with direct interface between administration and the citizenry. But by embracing the entire citizenry, on the one hand, and in contrast to classic liberalism, regarding all issues as public policy issues, on the other, the communitarian ideal founders. Fifth, we conclude this chapter with a brief foreshadowing of the need for our discourse theory.

I. The Loop Model of Democracy

It is widely assumed that in the United States the people are sovereign. Policy reflects their wishes. It is supposed to work like this:

1. The people are aware of what they want or need.
2. Competing candidates (or parties) for electoral office—political entrepreneurs—offer alternative packages of wants or needs that can be satisfied by particular methods.
3. People choose a representative by voting which alternative package seems to best match their preferences.
4. Coalitions of winning entrepreneurs pass laws reflecting the people's choice.
5. A vigilant populace pays enough attention to the process and the results to judge the elected representatives as either successful or wanting.
6. If satisfied with the results, people will reward incumbents with their votes; if unsatisfied, they will vote for alternative entrepreneurs offering alternative packages.

Although less purely democratic than direct democracy, in which the people would both make and implement policy (government *of* the people and *by* the people), the above process is often judged to be the best we can get in a complex mass society (see Bachrach, 1967). Although others act *for* the people, they are accountable *to* the people through the ballot box. The ballot symbolizes the political side of the politics-policy/administration dichotomy. On the administration side are hierarchy and chain of command, enabling elected officials to both control nonelected career officials and superintend their carrying out of the people's will. Because they are not themselves elected, administrators must be neutral malleable tools so that elected officials, who embody the will of the people, can have their way and be held accountable by the people for whatever does or does not get done.

A. EVIDENCE THAT THE LOOP IS MYTHICAL

Certain unpleasant realities of contemporary American political life place the electoral democratic accountability loop in doubt (see Parenti, 1983; Pateman, 1970). By the numbers:

1. The wants and needs of the people are, by and large, manipulated. There is no independent, popular will formation. News media, especially the electronic media from which most of the population gets its information, are managed more with an eye to entertain and titillate, to grab attention and sell air time to advertisers, than to politically inform.

2. Candidates for office rarely compete on the basis of complex policy alternatives. Image is much more important than substance. Negative campaigning and the manipulation of such symbols as change, flags, or Black rapists are today's state of the art. On campaign staffs, public relations gurus, advertising consultants, and style coaches are more important than policy analysts.

3. People do not vote for candidates on the basis of specific public policies, rationally considered. Majorities of the people often do not vote at all. Even if they did, a single-district, winner-take-all, two-party electoral system is an extremely blunt instrument for registering the people's specific policy preferences (Duverger, 1955; Page & Brody, 1972; see Prewitt, 1970, on voters' ineffectiveness in municipal elections). It is highly unlikely that a particular politician represents a particular constituent across the entire panoply of complex issues facing the nation. Single-issue voting further decreases the likelihood that the daily votes of legislators are inspired by the discipline of the electoral process. Those with more than one interest might get what they want on abortion or gun control, but not on capital gains or farm support. Indeed, it is mathematically impossible for "the people" to be represented on the entire concatenation of issues that affect their lives when choice is forced through the binary and centrist narrows of our electoral system.

4. After elections, coalitions of political entrepreneurs are more likely to be influenced by lobbyists and special interest associations; the pressure group system is bolstered by the politician-entrepreneur's need for campaign contributions, speaking honoraria, or well-funded ad campaigns (Blumenthal, 1980). Nor does voting on the basis of party assure particular policy stances. Coalitions that do momentarily gel produce incoherent policy because they are contrived contingently to attract a legislative majority. Am-

biguous, contradictory, and confused mandates will then plague the bureaucracy as it tries to figure out *which* politically generated command to neutrally implement.

5. If eternal vigilance is the price of liberty, only radio talk show hosts seem willing to pay it. Americans frequently do not know their representatives' names, much less their positions and their policy successes or failures. Vigilance is a 30-second TV spot excoriating opponents out of context.

6. It does not seem to matter that people are generally dissatisfied with the performance of Congress; they will reelect their own member. Instead, calls for term limits resonate across the electorate.

The above examples are drawn from the sphere of national politics, but we would assert that most of state and local politics would fit the generalization. State and local electoral politics are virtually devoid of competition on specific policy initiatives. Council elections are fought over who is the best "family man." Many local governmental units in mass suburbia have been captured by various factions of real estate developer interests, if not by the local economic powerhouse.

Now, we do not want to be interpreted as asserting that because the loop leaks at every joint, and electoral politics is but symbolism removed from political events, that therefore there is no democratic accountability in the United States. We would not go quite that far in our critique. We do want to maintain that politics and public policy are subject to much more diffuse and multilateral influences than can be explained by the electoral democratic accountability loop. We also want to maintain that, along with the self-interested influences rehearsed above, democracy flows from either side of the politics/administration dichotomy (which should now be thought of as a heuristic device). Robert Dahl (1971) and Charles Lindblom (1977) have insisted that this system be called *polyarchy* instead of *democracy*.

If policy directives do not flow in a direct channel from the people through elected officials, what of the otherwise unjustifiable top-down command structure? This command-and-control apparatus has been imposed on public administration practice in the name of the sovereign people, but when the loop fails or is connected to interests other than the people, the command structure loses much of its *raison d'être*. If the above analysis is even partly accurate, the people's name is being taken in vain. It is imperative that we affirm sources of bureaucratic accountability, but we will not find them in the "loop."

B. THE FOLLY OF BINDING BEHAVIOR BY WRITING RULES

The staying power of classical orthodoxy is attributable to its logical consistency and coherence. It is a tight interlocking system. So it was that when Carl Friedrich in 1940 suggested the necessity of discretion, Herman Finer (1941/1972) objected that bureaucratic discretion is tantamount to the theft of popular sovereignty. When bureaucrats independently exercise governmental power, they are also independently defining the public interest which, in Finer's view, only the public through its elected representatives (the loop) has the right to do. It followed that nonelected officials should be tightly controlled by an iron cage of rules, regulations, and standard operating procedures. We have already seen the weaknesses of the loop, but even if it were fully operational, rules cannot work as Finer hoped they could. Four arguments may be adduced: (a) rules beget more rules; (b) the vagaries of language make it an inadequate instrument for precisely controlling bureaucratic behavior; (c) in many cases the more rules there are, the less they control behavior; and (d) externally generated rules are associated with dysfunctions such as goal displacement, creaming, and working to rule.

Policy makers and executives at the pinnacle of hierarchies exercise control via promulgation of rules—in pathological bureaucracies. When subordinates' behaviors do not correspond to the original expectations, chiefs then pass down more rules as a corrective. Soon rules contradict one another, so clarifying rules are articulated, and so on. But the human capacity to find loopholes, or to be overly literal in interpreting commands will outrace management's ability to correct. Socrates said, "Such men are surely the most charming of all, setting down laws . . . always thinking they'll find some limit to wrongdoing . . . ignorant that they are really cutting off the heads of a Hydra" (Plato, *Republic,* Book IV, 426e, cited in Fox & Cochran, 1990).

It may be laid down as a general proposition that human behavior is too varied and rich to be specified or contained in written protocols. Meticulously articulated detail, comprehensiveness, or specificity is to no avail. The fundamental reason for this is that language itself is inadequate to the task. Languages are systems of generalizations built out of similes and metaphors; they capture life only in the abstract. At the very best they may accurately map the contours of life, but they cannot reproduce every rise and gully, nor the minute variations in ecosystems. Language has the marvelous capacity of defining figure from ground, but in doing so it cannot simultaneously display without contradiction all possible figures contained within the ground.

Correspondingly, the more rules there are, the more must implementers *choose* a particular concatenation of them to attend to. The paradigm case is street-level police who work in a community with 200 years of encrusted ordinances. Enforcing the spitting-on-the-sidewalk ordinance may have to be neglected in favor of ridding the streets of drunk drivers and car thieves. In situations like welfare eligibility casework, there may be so many rules, regulations, and interpretations of them as to allow wide latitude to the personal quirks of particular caseworkers (see Lipsky, 1980). Welfare policy will vary de facto from one corner of the building to another (Moore, 1987). The application of a rule to a case involves interpretation and judgment that are not specifiable (Beiner, 1983).

Finally, as has been documented (for instance) in the literature of job analysis, the attempt to specify exactly what must be done is an invitation to workers to do only that which is specified. Ignore all those important but unspecifiable aspects of competent job performance. So widespread is this tendency that it has several names: goal displacement, creaming, working to rule, and perverse measurement (Fox, 1991). In the process, employees are made sullen and resentful by rule-driven attempts to appraise performance and evaluate programs.

Does all this mean that there should be no rules? What about our cherished formula that we are a nation "governed by laws, not men"? An example from child rearing comes to mind. We get tied up in knots if we try to specify to our children complex codes of behavior. The best strategy seems to be to find the appropriate level of abstraction. "Be nice to your friends" works better than a infinite list of "don'ts" to cover every occasion. Inside the broad boundaries of the agreed standard "be nice" there will be, alas, much discretion; reciprocal moral education will occur over its exercise. Our discourse theory of governance contains just such broad rules, which we call "warrants for discourse" (see Chapter 5). But this is not the mainstream response to the crisis of democratic accountability called forth by the obvious dysfunctions of representative democracy. Reform efforts presuppose the validity of precisely what is wrong.

II. Quixotic Mainstream Reforms

It is not as if the problems of the loop model of representative democracy have gone completely unnoticed by scholars and writers. There have been calls to return to "strong" or "thick" democracy, which we associate with the communitarian tendency to be addressed below (in Section V of this chapter and in Chapter 3). The dominant tendency of those who recognize the problems, though, has been to reaffirm orthodoxy as an ideal and promote various reforms that might come closer to realizing the ideal. To the most influential of these writers—Mosher (1982) in public administration, Burke (1986) in public administration ethics, and Lowi (1979) in political science—the thought of abandoning legislative superiority based on popular sovereignty is . . . unthinkable. Lowi, in particular, has been critical of what he calls the second republic, which features legislatures relinquishing authority to agency bureaucrats who then form unholy alliances with special interests in their regulatory purview. This founds the literature of iron triangles and agency capture. Lowi would return to the first republic, where the legislative branch reasserts its authority.

Such a stance suggests the search for institutional reforms that would put us on the path back to the legislative supremacy of the first republic. If representatives are insufficiently representative of their constituencies, then we need to make it easier for the constituents to vote (motor voter law). If representatives use the power of their incumbency to garner disproportionate campaign war chests so that devious and venal media campaigns can be purchased, then we need campaign finance reform and term limitations. Much time, ink, pundit mindspace and political capital are spent pursing these procedural adjustments, but to what effect? Making it easier to vote may increase voter registration counts or stem the decline of such counts, but not by much. Besides, although Democrats count this as to their advantage, to increase the percentage of those who will vote because voting is easy is to increase the influence of the volatile and generally unreflective voter: another step toward plebiscitary democracy. As to campaign finance reform, experience teaches that the most likely result will be to relocate the loopholes. Term limitations actually delimits popular will. In sum, toying with procedural mechanisms seems to be a futile and quixotic exercise. Patching up leaks in one portion of the loop only increases the volume squirting through others. As we will be suggesting, procedural maladjustments are only symptoms of a more fundamental postmodern malady.

Halfhearted, crowd/poll-pleasing pseudo-reforms on the politics side are exceeded by the same instinct on the administration side. A brief excursion into the currently fashionable problematic of public administration ethics, and the relatively recent civil service reform, shows the difficulties of trying to reform the system when wearing the blinders of the loop understanding of democracy. Both examples represent conservative attempts to corral government by hobbling career public servants and bringing them, à la Finer, under closer control by elected politicians and their political appointees. These efforts are, in turn, justified as exercises in popular sovereignty. We want to display now the congruence between the loop model, which we disparage, and the attempt to make bureaucrats more ethical.

A. ETHICS REFORM

The classical model of public administration has an ethics (cf. Plant, 1983), although it is more often tacit than expressed (Ingersoll & Adams, 1992). In the language of academic moral philosophy, it is basically a utilitarian or consequentialist system. It possesses a definition of the good, albeit a provisional one. There is a foundational principle by which the good is supposed to be derived, and a theory of obligation incumbent on individual administrators. We call it the ethics of authoritative command.

1. The Good

Utilitarianism was designed by early 20th century progressives (see T. L. Cooper, 1991, pp. 110-111). The ethics of authoritative command adheres to the phrase "the greatest good for the greatest number." In the Benthamite philosophy from which it arises, *good* and *happiness* are words used to denote a positive ratio of pleasure to pain. Notice that this is not a very precise nor substantive view of the good; it is open-ended. Benefits must exceed costs. Gain must exceed pain. This open-ended specification of end values leads logically to a procedural view of how good and happiness are to be achieved. One is able to avoid defining in any substantive way what "good" consists of. Utilitarianism cannot tell you where to head but can only provide you with a measurement process that might be of some use. This is the logic of procedural utilitarianism. The greatest good will be achieved if proper procedures are followed.

2. Derived From the People

Lacking a firm grasp of exactly what happiness is, we should leave it to individuals to decide. In large part they should be free from government to pursue happiness by their own initiative in civil society. Insofar as happiness requires communal arrangements (because we are dealing with collective goods), pursuit of happiness must take place democratically by majority rule.

"Good" will be what we decide democratically to do in order to promote happiness. This view can generate considerable rhetorical power, as Oliver North discovered when he ran afoul of it. As Senator George Mitchell explained to North during the Iran-Contra hearings, "the American people have a right to be wrong," by which he meant that when the legislature shifts policy, no matter how whimsical it might appear, what used to be wrong is now right, whereas what was right is now wrong. The people (via their representatives) are the standard, the sovereign. There is no higher standard by which they may be judged wrong.

3. Role of the Individual Administrator

By this logic, impeccably deduced by Finer (1941/1972), bureaucrats qua bureaucrats are not to have wills of their own, although they may participate in will formation through delimited political activity (i.e., by voting). Bureaucrats are to shed their role in will formation once they pass through the doors of their bureaus. There, in return for security, they are to be functionaries carrying out legitimated commands from each level of superordination up to the representatives of the people, and thence supposedly to the attentive people at the ready to approve or disapprove with their votes. There is a neat correspondence between functional role that promotes efficiency[2] and ethical role. Both require obedience to rules and to supervisors who bear the authoritative interpretation of rules (Appleby, 1949). The point is that individual ethical choice is limited to choosing to follow the rules (the ethical thing to do) or to violate them by commission or omission (unethical acts). Without hierarchical accountability, the people would be deprived of the procedures to express their sovereignty and hence their current definition of the greatest good for the greatest number.

4. Current Manifestations

The ethics of authoritative command is the way students of ethics would describe the traditional progressivist model of public administration. Orthodoxy shares with the ethics of authoritative command certain strengths and weaknesses. The major strengths lie in the fact that it is still the basic official institutional view—it is legitimate. Although the traditional progressivist model—orthodoxy and its sovereignty loop—is tattered and weakened, it has not been replaced by some new coherent vision. As it is the unquestioned presupposition, or foundational myth, of elected officials, the press, textbook political science, and the American Society for Public Administration (Mertins & Hennigan, 1982, p. 41), it is not surprising that much of what is currently classified as ethics follows from it. Using the means available to them, the passing of laws and promulgation of regulations, officials attempt to reinforce ethical behavior by making rules that are basically designed to ensure that the other rules are followed. Some people have been unethical in that they have not followed rules. Therefore sanctions against those who violate rules must be made more stringent, and the temptations to violate rules must be removed. Hence the U.S. Office of Government Ethics was established to administer the ethics of authoritative command. The characteristic case for this ethics is conflict of interest. One is pulled away from neutrality by a magnetic force, such as money wielded by special interests. We remove that force by making it illegal (ban accepting gifts), censurable (via legislative ethics committees), or difficult to cash in on (legislation against "revolving doors," that is, immediate employment by an entity over which one once exercised regulatory power).

We submit that if the logic of the loop model and its rule elaboration corollary is as flawed as we maintain, attempts to fix it by ethics reform are quixotic. Ethics legislation and more rules cannot curb the necessary exercise of discretion; they can only make its exercise doubly blameworthy. Ethics rules are added to all the other rules proactive policy makers/implementers cannot avoid violating in the everyday carrying out of their functions. When they do violate one, they have also violated the ethics rule against violating rules. Administrative life becomes more and more like staying in good graces with an Indonesian *jupen* (uniformed officer of the ministry of information). With so many ways to misbehave, blame can always be affixed by anyone offended by any other's creed, personal style, or mode of expression. Far from removing personalism, the overarticulation of rules ensures it.

B. CIVIL SERVICE REFORM

It is more than coincidental that the act establishing the U.S. Office of Government Ethics was passed the same year as the Civil Service Reform Act of 1978. Both occurred at the trough of the decline in governmental legitimacy. This is traceable, we contend, to deficiencies in contemporary American representative democracy. Both ethics reform and personnel reform reassert the loop model in a futile attempt to solve problems created by attachment to the model itself.

Civil service reform had been on the agenda of executive-level reformers in and out of government since the Second Hoover Commission in the early fifties (Dillman, 1984, pp. 206-209; Knott & Miller, 1987, pp. 240-247). A major goal was to bring the bureaucracy to bay by rethinking civil service regulations that hindered the disciplining of putatively recalcitrant public servants. The fortuitous confluence of economic recession (stagflation), tax revolt, the diminished legitimacy of governmental institutions that accompanied the Watergate scandal, and certain policy failures, such as the Vietnam war and the war on poverty, created an accommodating climate for accomplishment of the reforms. Despite the fact that blame for these events can be more properly laid at the door of political elites, career civil servants were the ones targeted for retribution. Indeed, by 1978, bureaucrat bashing had become so much a part of the political campaign spectacle that in a Gallup poll over 60% of the American public agreed that "federal government employees do not work as hard as they would in nongovernment jobs," that "the federal government employs too many people," and that "federal workers are paid more than they would earn in nongovernmental jobs." Jimmy Carter, in proposing his legislation, opined: "The public suspects that there are too many government workers, that they are underworked, overpaid and insulated from the consequences of incompetence" (U.S. Senate, 1978, pp. 243-244).

Although there were many aspects to civil service reform, performance appraisal was the most important, in the sense that it embodied the punitive and scientistic crusade (Fox, 1991; Thayer, 1978). Simply put, performance appraisal was the key to enhanced managerial control. In its first publication, the newly established Office of Personnel Management made no bones about its goals:

> Perhaps the key problem in the past few years in public personnel administration has been the lack of responsiveness of career personnel to the needs of management. . . . The dominant theme in public personnel reform is to improve the responsiveness of civil service personnel to management and hence to the general public to which management [not the whole service?!] is ultimately accountable. (U.S. Office of Personnel Management, 1979, p. 1)

Resuscitated by the stroke of Jimmy Carter's pen was the classical panoply of questionable assumptions about the nature of work and management in the public sector, including the intellectually tattered politics/administration dichotomy (compare Ban & Ingraham, 1984, p. 2). Again, nonelected public servants must be tightly controlled, in this case by assessing performance in relation to management goals. These goals themselves supposedly are derived from law, passed by elected officials who in turn are blessed by popular will.

Were democracy more like a discourse, the fatuous connection between the politicians' malfeasance and the resulting tightening of control mechanisms on civil servants who were not to blame would not stand.

We have argued that adherence to the loop model leads to both bad ethics and bad personnel policy. There is no room in this tightly knit command-and-control logic for ethical individuals holding public jobs to exercise the autonomy integral for organizational performance. To be wedded to the loop is to be unable to transcend Taylorist management styles.

Starkly put, the loop model allows us to don the mantle of democracy only if we are dictators at the worksite. Obversely, to be democrats at the worksite is to steal sovereignty. The discomfort of this postulate promotes theorizing by students of public administration.

III. The Institutionalist/Constitutionalist Alternative

The incredulity of representative democracy is both a curse and an opportunity. It is a curse on public administration because it deprives it of access to popular sovereignty as it is popularly misunderstood. Our (we in public administration) political masters exhibit behaviors associated with charlatans and demagogues, and sometimes crooks, parading under the false but garish banner of the will of the people. The intellectual misgivings associated with representative democracy provide an opportunity because sovereignty itself may be redefined to include public administration, but only if it can be made democratic in some new (nonelectoral) sense. To date, the two dominant responses to this paradigm anxiety have been constitutionalism and citizen activation. Both owe their respective structures to the requirements of legitimacy and accountability. The first substitutes the Constitution for the electoral victors of the moment. Here loyalty to the sovereign people need not be compromised if it can be shown that constitutional principles have primacy over the merely elected. From the motley crew shouting conflicting orders, we may choose which ones to obey when guided by the constitutional founding. The second seeks to bypass the electoral loop by going directly to the sovereign citizens. Here we are instructed to replace electoral, representative weak democracy with direct strong democracy. We turn first to an exploration of the constitutionalist alternative.

Constitutionalism means different things in different contexts and literatures. Here the term is used to identify a class of arguments now sufficiently solidified and complete to qualify as an alternative theory vying to replace orthodoxy in public administration. The leading intellectual proponent of constitutionalism in this sense is John Rohr. His case for refounding public administration based on a particular reading of the founding is all the more influential as the cornerstone of the Blacksburg manifesto (Wamsley, 1990, p. 23) and as the template for various interpretations from D. F. Morgan (1990) to Spicer and Terry (1993). As the impressively erudite Rohr is an unlikely man of straw, it is Rohr's (1986) argument which merits explication and critique.

A. ROHR'S THESIS

Rohr is straightforward: "The purpose of this book is to legitimate the administrative state in terms of constitutional principle" (Rohr, 1986, p. ix). But how can Public Administration (capitalized here in acquiescence to the convention of Blacksburg scholars) be a constitutionally legitimate governmental structure in its own right when the word *administration* appears nowhere in the written Constitution? Rohr's answer is that a constitution is more than the particular contract which the document codifies. A constitution is a covenant (p. x). Given the religious overtones of *covenant,* Rohr here seems to mean that a contract is the letter, whereas a covenant is the spirit, of an agreement between two or more parties. But how may one "read" the spirit? Rohr's answer is that it should be read through the exegesis of writings of those engaged in the argument (p. 9), exegesis being the critical interpretation of text. For Rohr, this exegesis has as its object an expanded text including the actual Constitution, *The Federalist Papers,* and writings of the antifederalists as well. The purpose of exegesis is to distill larger, more fundamental verities from the clutter of impassioned points made by debaters in the heat of the moment. In such context the constitutional document itself is only the provisional synthesis, a strong but not decisive point held in tension in the larger agonistic web of argumentation and counterargument.

Constitutional in this sense is certainly a more encompassing concept than the crabbed constitution of the strict constructionist jurist. Constitutionalism as a legitimizing font for the administrative state is really about the founding. "The Constitution is the symbol of the founding of the Republic and in politics, 'foundings' are normative" (Rohr, 1986, p. 7). "The source of authority of regimes is the founding act itself" (p. 179). But what is a *founding*? In the history of political philosophy, many watershed thinkers revere foundings. To Plato, for instance, if the ideal of the Republic cannot be actualized, the second best state is one of laws stemming from a founding. Similarly, Rousseau settles for the founding acts of a Legislator, failing the emergence of institutional manifestations of the general will. Social contract theory in general—Hobbes, Locke, and recently Rawls—imagines some founding moment when for various reasons the people come together to create unabrogatable arrangements for living together in (at least) peace, if not justice and harmony. Rohr suggests that this second-best *historicism* is what he has in mind. By such logic, foundings may approximate to varying degrees Absolute Justice/Truth. Although they are a compromise from Absolute Justice, and they differ from place to place and time to time (such differences already a regrettable move along the spectrum from ideal to appearance), these approximations usually depend on the sagacity of the humans (or suffer from the lack thereof) who serve as the vehicles of Truth or Justice. In the case of the founding of the American republic, though, there is not one wise solon-like law maker; there is instead a formidable committee, whose members argue. Rohr's innovation, then, is to embody the founding not in a founder, nor even the founding fathers. Rather, the founding is in the thoughts and principles flowing between the participants and between them and their interlocutors. "The founding was in the argument" (p. 179).[3] Thus when we swear an oath to protect the Constitution we swear to honor the founding and the tradition coalesced by that act, we swear to honor the argument, and in a sense we swear also to engage ourselves in the argument, bounded by the high principles through which it was originally conducted.[4]

So how is all this founding talk related to the Public Administration? Rohr (1986) makes three modest claims: "The administrative state is consistent with the Constitution, fulfills its design, and heals a longstanding major defect" (p. 13). First, although the Public Administration exercises executive, legislative, and judicial powers, it does not violate the relaxed standard of separation of powers, which standard may be adduced from the founding argument. Second, the Public Administration provides a constitutional "balance wheel" originally assigned to the nonelected Senate. Third, the Public Administration provides a measure of (demographic) representation insufficiently fulfilled by the strictly constitutional branches.

B. CRITIQUE OF CONSTITUTIONALISM

We have tried to portray constitutionalism with the genuine sympathy we feel for it and the cause which it champions. Constitutional legitimacy for government's embattled regulars surely is worth the effort. The Blacksburg manifesto, which relies on constitutional legitimacy, resonates with a dignity deserved by dedicated public servants in the agencies. As the first coordinated

effort to replace dysfunctional public administration orthodoxy, the manifesto blazes a path that subsequent efforts will gratefully follow before they
too face the undergrowth, but using machetes whose edges have been spared
the dulling effects of the first cut.

Ultimately constitutionalism fails us because it is simply too conservative;
it is reactionary in the noble but still fettering Burkean sense. To defend the
administrative state by constitutional inquiry looks back instead of forward.
The attempt to save the administrative state from the attacks of primitive
libertarian philistines fights the battle on the wrong ground. One ends up
forced to affirm many arrangements that merit, instead, transformation.
Forced by the right-wing contras to a desperate redoubt, one finds oneself
fighting alongside such past and future nemeses as hierarchy, moribund
institutional boundaries, agency aggrandizement (see, e.g., Kronenberg's
1990 challenge), and all the other bureau pathologies many of us had once
hoped to transcend. As the Blacksburg scholars admit (Wamsley et al., 1990,
preface), they have come to embrace institutionalism and authority at least
as a welcome alternative to the libertarian anarchy of the resurgent right. We
contend that this is overly defeatist. Defense of the status quo robs public
administration theorists of the independence required to imagine more emancipating conditions of work and governance. We should instead be alert to
seize upon emerging trends and to coax from them more authentic human
interrelationships. Many niggling quarrels—such as the exclusion of dedicated state and local civil servants, the elitism implied by the role of the
"upper reaches" of the civil service for which Rohr proposes a senatorial
role—could (but won't) be picked. Other more substantive objections which
we share with others (such as Stivers's 1993 charge of instrumentalism of
the founders, or P. Cooper's 1990 demur relating to agencies' actual performance) need not be repeated here. Constitutionalism (and *to the degree* of its
reliance on same, the Blacksburg initiative[5]) ought not be afforded pride of
place in the colloquy for an alternative model because it stoops to defensive
and tortured argumentation; lacks a solid referent; and seems too closely
tied, by virtue of the institutionalism implied, to given structures of
governance.

1. Tortured Argumentation

One cannot but admire the careful constitutional scholarship and the many
hours of meticulous reading that Rohr (1986) exhibits in his *To Run a
Constitution*. Few would agree to duel with him on these, his, grounds. He

is also scrupulously honest about the results of these labors. The strongest case he can make for constitutional legitimacy of the Public Administration remains, by his admission, weak. Rohr would not ask for relaxed standards of judgment, or poetic license (pp. 174-178), were it not so. Because the cause—defending embattled bureaucrats—is just, we are asked to suspend normal protocols of scholarly argumentation. Aristotle's dictum that no more precision should be required than a subject admits is invoked to justify this suspension. At one point (p. 176) novelty by itself stands as a criterion for positive evaluation of the argument. Even granting all such dispensations, in the end it is not so much that the Constitution founds the Public Administration, as it is that the Public Administration is not inconsistent with it. But by that logic, the Public Administration is no less legitimate than, *tu quoque,* the imperial presidency, an activist judiciary, or, heaven forbid, the corps of Washington lobbyists. For such diluted product, we think Rohr asks too dear a price. For violating the separation of powers, we are urged to adopt the most relaxed standards that can be read from Publius. For the independence to obey whichever master the Public Administration deigns to hear, we are asked to acquiesce to the analogy of a long since abandoned senatorial structure and its metaphoric balance wheel. The reasoning, although not exactly fallacious, nonetheless fails to persuade. An equally serious difficulty is what we call the riddle of the vanishing referent.

2. Vanishing Referent

The regime norms from which American bureaucrats are urged to deduce their ethics (Rohr, 1989) are vanishing referents (Fox, 1993). Like mirages and rainbows, they disappear when approached. So too seems the case with the cluster of concepts: Constitution, principle, covenant, contract, tradition, founding and the argument. In Rohr's text they are tautologically defined only in relation to each other. They take the form: What is X? It is Y. What is Y? It is Z. What is Z? It is X. (For example, what are constitutional values? They are regime values. What are regime values? They are the polity. What is the polity? That political entity that was brought into being by the ratification of the Constitution.) Like the classic caricature of a bureaucratic runaround, one is endlessly transferred to the next office without satisfaction. Specifically, if the Constitution owes its validity not to the document so named, but to a founding, and if the founding enacted a covenant that was itself based on the principles which bounded the argument, how can anything substantive about it be confidently asserted? Or indeed, with a little interpretive creativity, virtually anything could be audaciously asserted. If one is dissatisfied with the results of straightforward Constitution reading, just expand the parameters of the argument. How far from the framers and signers can we go? If we consult the antifederalists on the left, as Rohr does, should we exclude British loyalists on the right? If so, on what principle of exclusion? Should we not also consult (say) the recently unearthed diaries of unindicted co-conspirators of Shay's and the Whiskey rebellions? And what nominal time frame brackets the founding? Are we not still founding when we take the oath to uphold and support the argument? The point, overly made, is that constitutional legitimacy is a chimera wrapped in an enigma.

3. Institutionalism

What effect does the attempt to ground the Public Administration in the Constitution have on the self-proclaimed neoinstitutionalism of the Blacksburg manifesto? We believe that it introduces a certain gravity, a weight, that ends up overmuch affirming given institutions, or worse, institutions as given. This, in turn, leads to a "hardening of the categories," reminiscent of the old discredited institutionalism where primacy of scholarly attention was granted to structures over functions, written formal arrangements over informal actual practices, and manifest truisms over latent realities.

The institutionally grounded "Minnowbrook" (that is, a radical departure from mainstream public administration that nonetheless retains administrative traditions) claimed by the Blacksburg scholars (Wamsley et al., 1990) may be possible, but there is the danger of an institutionally cemented Minnowbrook. Thinking in constitutional terms focuses attention on such institutional categories as powers of the presidency, where tax bills originate, who makes war, who confirms treaties, whether or not a president can fire a Senate-approved cabinet officer, and so on. Thinking in such terms leads the mind along well-worn paths, among the monuments and museums of official Washington, D.C. Political science as a discipline abandoned such an approach two revolutions ago, and for good reason. That tough-minded generation of scholars returning from World War II to be trained on the GI Bill were not convinced that the hypostatized reality described by constitutions had much to do with politics as it was experienced. Students of comparative politics were particularly alienated by the attempt to describe the differences between Argentina and the Soviet Union in terms of their constitutions. More radically inclined Americanists found power everywhere, constrained hardly at all by constitutional niceties. Institutional codes were not the banks that contained the river of power, but only outcroppings around, over, and through which it flowed. If powerful robber barons wanted to overwhelm state-level qualms about them, the Constitution accommodated them by construing corporations to be individuals with rights. If corporations felt threatened by nationalist politicians in Third World countries, the Constitution did not prevent U.S. military intervention on their behalf. If, as Rohr (1993, p. 246) writes, the founding period is normative for American politics and that is just a *fact,* why do Americans tolerate normatively objectionable practices, such as negative, deceitful, political campaigning? From whence arise these other normative political standards, such as winning the election at all cost? The first political science revolution away from institutionalism was the unfortunate behavioral one, but that should not blind us to the inadequacies of what was left behind; good riddance. That the second (postbehavioral) revolution was toward a policy orientation (for service in which Wamsley, for one, has been deservedly decorated) and not back to institutionalism, is a development that should not go unremarked.

Now it is true that there is at least a fad for neoinstitutionalism in political science. But the mediating influence of institutions can be fresh news only to economists. The point of it seems to be that institutions influence behavior and that this influence is underemphasized by behavioralism, liberal individualism, and the mathematicians of *homo economicus.* One would hope that these truths would quickly ascend to the status of self-evident so that one would not have to join a neoinstitutionalist school to be counted as one who affirms them. Otherwise, constitutional-institutionalism fetters inquiry when excessive attention is paid it. It biases our thought and skews our perceptual lens back to what organization theory now disdains as the closed system approach. We believe that we would be better off to cease conceptualizing institutions as either entities (à la institutionalism) or reified events (à la the founding), and instead learn to see overlapping consecutions (sequences or iterations) of phenomenological practices which evince varying degrees of stability (and, one might add, relevance, merit, and validity).

Helpful here is Giddens's (1984) structuration theory in developing a framework that transcends institutions while at the same time, by grounding social structures in social relations, it discerns the special influences of institutions. We use the structuration approach in articulating (in Chapter 4) the concept of energy fields, which we employ to account for the effects of institutional and habitual-cultural sediments on behavior, while avoiding reifying particular formal institutions. Structuration theory allows one to assay the behavior-channeling practices that make up what are called institutions and to see the institution-like practices in their nascent social formations. Some of these institution-like but not-fully-institutionalized practices that are of particular interest in Chapter 5 include interagency consortia, agency-transcending policy networks and subsystems, intergovernmental and interjurisdictional task forces, adhocracies, citizen-agency coproduction and informal social-political networks. We are ill-served if the model that ends up replacing orthodoxy neglects its role as midwife to the emancipating potentials of the future for the sake of legitimizing the past and the given. It is the pursuit of the public interest, not a historical episode, that legitimates the efforts of all who join with proactive public administrators, sometimes across institutional lines, in that endeavor. This last sentence, in addition to expressing our views, could have been written by someone disposed toward the citizen/communitarian tendency.

IV. Communitarian/Citizen Alternative

The other major contender to replace orthodoxy is citizen activation or civism. Like the authors of this contribution, communitarians would not be primarily concerned about the legitimacy of given institutions as constitutional/neoinstitutionalists are. However, in public administration, the legitimacy crisis is their entrée to the discourse caused by paradigm anxiety. As communitarianism is an essentially premodern philosophy, it has never been seen to illicitly associate with the utility-maximizing individualism that is presupposed by the loop model. The weakness of representative democracy represents, for communitarians, an opportunity to resuscitate the direct democracy of the community. Although the agencies that Blacksburg scholars would affirm may exhibit characteristics of community, their hierarchical structure and rigid turf-protectionist boundaries would surely be anathema to contemporary communitarians. Communitarians want strong democracy that leads to justice. People should be involved in the decisions that affect their lives, not only for the sake of justice, but also because the full development of their human potential requires it. People must involve themselves in the community to escape from the modern alienation that would otherwise typify their lives. Communitarians, then, would also question the neoinstitutionalism and constitutionalism of the first-mentioned alternative to orthodoxy. The full development of human potential in community takes precedence over archaic constitutional debates and the current agential manifestations of these debates. Moreover, if the loop model is as dysfunctional as has been claimed, a logical alternative is to bypass the masters of ill-begotten political superordination and make common cause with the citizens themselves.

If the constitutional model harkens back to a sacred founding of the republic, citizen-administration solidarity harkens back to the direct democracy of the Athenian polis, the Swiss canton, and the New England town. Citizen engagement is both more diffusely defined than constitutionalism and possessed of a more complete standpoint. It is diffuse because unlike Blacksburg figures, its adherents (among which we count Adams et al., 1990; Chandler, 1984; T. L. Cooper, 1991; Fredrickson, 1982; Gawthrop, 1984; and Stivers, 1990a) are scattered and have not sat down to define their areas of agreement. It is a more thorough standpoint insofar as those advocating the citizen approach either implicitly or explicitly base their view on communitarianism. Communitarianism itself is a full-blown philosophical school strongly rooted in ancient (Aristotle), medieval (St. Thomas Aquinas) and contemporary thought (e.g., Jonsen & Toulmin, 1988, MacIntyre, 1984; C. Taylor, 1985; and to a lesser extent Walzer, 1983). Readers may be familiar with Bellah, Madsen, Sullivan, Swidler, and Tipton's (1985) *Habits of the Heart* and Bellah et al.'s (1991) *The Good Society,* which are also rooted in communitarianism.

It might be helpful to briefly review the major tenets of philosophical communitarianism to see the power of it. Communitarianism can be portrayed in four steps making up Section B below. It has (a) a different (from modernist liberal, sometimes called classical liberal) view of the self, which (b) alters the locus and direction of agential causality, which (c) calls forth a teleology of virtue or character ethics, which in turn (d) promotes a praxis typified by *phronesis* (practical wisdom). Then, in section C: (a) difficulties with this standpoint will be adduced; (b) communitarian adjustments to account for these problems will be noted; and (c) the problem of citizen apathy, for which communitarians are insufficiently armed, will be introduced.

A. COMMUNITARIANISM: BEDROCK VIEW

1. The Self

The modern liberal understanding of the self supposes an atomistic (bourgeois) individual rationally maximizing valuables unto its lonely self. Communitarians protest that the "self" that such doctrines presuppose is hardly a recognizable self at all. Such a cipher self has no culture, no history, and no situatedness; it is not embodied. It is an abstract self, a disembodied reasoning being theoretically fashioned after Descartes's cogito: "I think, therefore I am." Obversely, communitarianism follows Aristotle's dictum that a person is a social/political animal, the full development of which can only occur in a well-ordered community (polis). This more robust self comes stamped by its past community experience and does not have the absolute free will assumed for abstract, atomistic, and autonomous individuals.

2. The Primacy of Community

Communitarians begin not with the atomistic sovereign individual but with context. "They view human agency as situated in a concrete moral and political context and stress the constitutive role that communal aims and attachments assume for a situated self" (d'Entreves, 1992, p. 180). Individuals, it follows, do not act as if in a vacuum. Causality—which in orthodox-liberal-modernist patterns runs from autonomous individual consciousness, to judgment or decision, to action—is now conceived by communitarians as a dialectical, reciprocal causality between individuals and the communal-historical context in which they have been formed. This context is already well-populated with significant others. Indeed, without context the human individual is unimaginable—there would be no perceivable physiognomy, no temperament, no character, no flash of personality. An important implication of this shift in locus is to elevate the community to, if not absolute primacy, at least coequal causal primacy. In orthodoxy, individual self-interest is assumed to be the primordial force in life, coordinated by the invisible hand of the market and tempered subsequently by an overlay of moral obligation dictated by right reason. In contrast, communitarians assume that the community itself and other humans are a precondition for human life and happiness. It follows that other-regardingness, altruism, loyalty, community attachments, and other group-based sentiments are not mere eccentric deviations from the norm of self-centered rationality, but are part of being in a human community. Attachments are not to be explained away as irrational exogenous factors. This communitarian view undermines rational choice theory and dominant branches of economics (for public policy implications see Stone, 1988).

3. Teleology of Virtue and Character

The cultivation of internal traits of character and virtue, then, are the goals of a well-ordered polis. Citizenship in a polis, by this view, is not simply a matter of convenient administration of affairs. Citizenship is a crucial part of the process of character cultivation. One does not emerge from the womb as a completely virtuous being nor suddenly become virtuous at puberty. Fully developed virtue and character, the telos of human life, require active participation in communal governance. The process of discourse with communal others, working out common ground, developing consensus, is essential to the full development of human potential. Humans are political animals not only out of material need, but for full spiritual maturation.

4. Phronesis

A well-ordered community of trust does not require rational-comprehensive social science. The latter, a mistake of the Enlightenment, assumes an impossible all-knowing God's-eye scan congruent only with predictable, rational, maximizing individuals and the negative freedom (that is, the rights and freedoms attached to classic liberalism; Berlin, 1979) entailed by that view. The looser but more realistic standards of *phronesis* (practical wisdom) are more suited to a discourse of communal citizens making decisions in concert. As Stivers (1990a) has written: "The restoration of an understanding of governance as the exercise of practical wisdom . . . involves moving . . . toward greater reliance on tentative strategies that self-correct through frequent feedback of information about their effects" (p. 260).

B. COMMUNITARIANISM: CRITICISMS AND RESPONSES

1. The Problems

Four overlapping problems quickly surface when one begins to think through communitarianism. If a major problem with orthodoxy is the assumption of autonomous individualism, an abstraction of real situated individuals, the parallel problem with communitarianism is the assumption that communities are wholly or largely benign. Communitarianism has totalitarian tendencies, in that all aspects of life are gathered up, as it were, by the teleological thrust toward well-ordered harmony. At best, people may find this insufferably boring. At worst, eccentricities would be construed by community fussbudgets as inconsistent with community goals—mind-numbing conformity becomes the price of membership. The rights to privacy afforded sovereign individuals and the separate spheres (i.e., work, leisure, family, religion) carved out by liberal pluralism may be abrogated in communitarianism for the sake of community integrity, morality, or unity. Remember, too, for every misty dream of bucolic rural community there is an equally compelling vision of the dead weight of conformity enforced by community elders (elites) and self-appointed casuistrists. The dilemma may be instantly grasped by replacing the word *state* for *community* in all preceding sentences. A related problem is that communitarianism may be essentially an idealistic stained-glass-window nostalgia no longer viable as a real option in the mass societies inexorably created by advanced and postindustrial capitalism, a condition further articulated in Chapter 3.

2. Adjustments to Base Communitarianism

The above difficulties of communitarianism have not gone unnoticed by its public administration champions. T. L. Cooper (1987, 1991) has tried to accommodate them by amendment. Acknowledging the incorrigible actuality of pluralism, Cooper avoids the nostalgia and totalitarian traps mentioned above. Adopting Cochran's (1982) innovative theoretical move, he conceptualizes community in pluralistic, associational terms, hence freeing community from the confinement of geographical jurisdiction. Thus rendered, community becomes more like an electronically augmented, communication-age affinity group. This allows communities with qualities similar to Tocqueville's voluntary associations to serve as mediating institutions between (merely) legal citizens and government. By *legal citizens* Cooper means minimalist citizenship consistent with atomistic passive individuals possessing the usual rights and freedoms—what Sir Isaiah Berlin (1979) aptly calls negative freedom. Within these associations lies the potential for communities. The communitarian milieu, where full ethical citizenship flourishes, is nurtured in these communities.

The citizen-administrator encourages these communities and dialectically intermingles with them. Adminstrators themselves are ethically nourished and cocreated within professional communities in government. (Stivers, 1990a, pp. 267ff. makes a similar point.) This sort of professionalism is distinguished from the sort of professionalism entailed by guild protectionism. That sort of professionalism has been criticized as a conspiracy against the laity, a self-serving professionalism illegitimately cooked up behind veils of expertise, technique, and credentialing. MacIntyre's (1984) distinction between internal and external goods of a practice is appropriated for the purpose of distinguishing between ethical professionalism and self-serving professionalism (Cooper, 1987). Professionalism must remain open to external influences. Created by this theoretical move is a complex array of overlapping communities synergistically cocreating ethical citizens, some of whom also will be ethical citizen-administrators in the virtue sense. As in Barber's (1984) strong democracy, not only would such a scheme provide for will formation and legitimate governance, but—more important to communitarians—it would also encourage the full development of human potential, which fulfills the teleological obligation to participate in community decisions that affect both the individual and the commonweal (Cochran, 1982, cited in T. L. Cooper, 1991, p. 160). We will adopt many of these amendments and coopt them as integral parts of discourse theory. Other adjustments cannot be abided.

Both Cooper and Stivers have anticipated a response to a class of objections that idealism of any sort is liable to attract. What is the response to the criticism that the existing state of affairs obviates deployment of the communitarian model? The answer is the "tension between the real and ideal" gambit. Stivers (1990a) has gone so far as to turn the lack of correspondence between real and ideal into a virtue:

> Unless we understand that our intentions—the ends for which the state was formed—are out of reach, we will be unable to practice the trust in one another that enables us to accept the inevitable imperfections of actual policies. (p. 254)

We can only point out that such a gambit can be used on behalf of any ideal. If we are going to imagine ideals validated by the distance of them from the existent, why not imagine one where the state has withered away, humans have transcended scarcity, labor is no longer forced by survival needs, and administration is over only things, not people? Why not dream beyond Marx of the *German Ideology* and the *Grundrisse* instead of dreaming only beyond Skinner of *Walden II*?

On the matter of citizen apathy, the communitarian ideal is especially problematic.

3. The Problem of Citizen Apathy

Communitarianism, we believe, stumbles over the problem of citizen apathy. Communitarians cannot abide indifference and inattention among the would-be citizenry. We, on the other hand, believe the apathetic have a right to their ways.

If most people are not much interested in matters of governance, the communitarian model would seem an unlikely proposition. Teenagers capable of infinitely varied and precise recognition of categories of sports shoes, trousers, and other fashions cannot name cabinet-level agencies. But before the hand wringing begins, a pause may be in order. Perhaps we are the arrogant ones, we professional political junkies, policy wonks, and government watchers. Imagine the range of human endeavor that we also neglect. Our close attention to issues of governance should not lead us to assume that others would be equally attentive if left to their own devices. Perhaps the communitarian fulfillment by the governmentally apathetic could come not from governing in the usual sense of self-government, but from participation in all the other myriad forms of self-through-community actualization available to them, including car racing, dog clubs, RV clubs, church activities, little leagues, fan clubs, gangs, and so on ad infinitum. Perhaps the comforting knowledge that one could at any time *become* active and have influence is enough democracy for the average middle-class citizen.

Furthermore, it is easy to make the *standpunkt* error of falsely conflating community governance with what our public administrationists' perspective has labeled governance. We have reified the term *governance,* confusing the given conception with the thing itself. Indeed, the usual and immediately apparent reaction to the juxtaposition of some form of ideal democracy, on the one hand, with evidence of citizen apathy, on the other, is to assume that apathy is unnatural and has been caused by some fundamental flaw in the political or societal structure. Further, we should strive to overcome this flaw, this apathy. This response is doubly seductive from the communitarian perspective, where participation is a necessary component of being human at all. To leave people alone with their apathy is to consign them to the status of *untermenschen.* If we do not wish to "force them to be free," would it be all right if we merely empower them (Adams et al., 1990)? Empowerment would bring into the community those citizens who have been shut out. Certain reforms flow from this view. Voter registration regulations should be reformed to make it easier to vote; policy analysis should avoid jargon so that normal citizens can understand the issues; sunshine legislation should be pursued to ensure that citizens have adequate access to information; public interest TV channels should be set up to counter the tendency for media to be monopolized or oligopolized in fewer and fewer hands. The theory of empowerment is behind the current, and laudable, experiment in Chicago to devolve previously centralized school board power to neighborhood boards. We urge strong and active support for all such measures, but it is our skeptical guess that they will not be able to significantly counterbalance the inertia of citizen inattention. Sunshine legislation and open hearings only made budgetary markup sessions more accessible to well-heeled and well-organized special interest groups, not to the citizenry at large. Giving citizens the theoretical capability of obtaining more information on top of the information they already ignore is not helpful to them. It is, however, helpful to the attentive citizens, those who engage their intellect, passion, and personal reputations with the issues, those who have earned warrants for discourse.

In a community where the general citizenry is inattentive except during crises or when malfeasance has become egregious, democracy may be *for* the people but it cannot be claimed that it is *of* or *by* the people. Mass democracy exists only as potential—a potential that should, of course, be preserved at all costs. For the remainder, we have a discourse of "citizens in lieu of the rest of us" (Walzer, 1970, quoted in T. L. Cooper, 1991). These are representative citizens, as well as citizen-administrators. It is the task of this book to suggest that the best democracy we can get in our postmodern mass consumer society is a discourse of the nonapathetic, of those citizens whose warrant for entry into the discourse is political intentionality. We must hasten to admit that we do not regard this solution as the ideally best one. For that, we too are communitarians. The difference is that for the here and now, the question is not so much what best fulfills human potential? (a question to which the communitarians have the best answer) as what should we do next? (a question for which discourse theory has been crafted).

V. The Need for Discourse Theory

The areas of agreement between the Blacksburg manifesto (taken as a whole, rather than reductively as an extension of constitutionalism), communitarianism, and our discourse theory are much greater than the differences. All of us are discretionists; we all hold the possibility of public administration acting in the public interest; we all seek to avoid technicism; we are all antipositivists; and we would all distance ourselves from the type of professionalism which is nothing more than guild protectionism. Then, too, with the Blacksburg group we would like to see some sort of social formation of sufficient density and strength to counter the worst aspects of monopoly capitalism. And along with public administrationist communitarians (Stivers, in particular) we are wary of drawing too-thick lines between public administration and the citizenry.

So why do we propose a different theory? For two reasons, really. First, we do not have (nor see the reasons for) the same commitment as either the Blacksburg group or public administration-type communitarians to legitimizing public administration per se. Nor, on the other side of the coin, are we as worried about the accountability of it to something external called sovereign. As radical nominalists, we think legitimacy is in the doing of something. For us the crucial question is not what legitimizes what we have done and are doing, but again, what should we do next? In a nominalist rendering of sovereignty, it is understood that the term dates back to medieval thinkers who sought a new ruse to replace the shopworn divine right of kings. In other words, sovereignty does not denote anything specifically. Sovereignty is but a maneuver in some strategically crafted argument, an attempt to legitimize and privilege one arrangement over some other imaginable arrangement.

The second reason is perhaps a preference of temperament. Autobiographically, as late-blooming working-class kids, we think neither that apathy is an unnatural state nor that government in the United States is so closed off that anyone with a little effort couldn't participate if he or she wanted to do so. We have hit upon discourse theory, conceptually linked to Habermas's work, as a way to overcome what we perceive to be the shortcomings of Blacksburg institutionalism and communitarianism. Discourse theory is a way to highlight the importance of the quality of policy deliberation. That is to say, we see no reason why serious participants in the public conversation need suffer fools, gadflies, extremists, plotters, ego trippers, or the greedy hiding behind sophistry, at least not gladly.

Perhaps we would not be such tough-minded agnostics were it not for our analysis of what ails the republic in the postmodern condition, to which we now turn.

Notes

1. This is not the place to gather up all critiques of orthodoxy. Hierarchy and scientific management have been savaged by vast literatures ranging from efficiency orientations of organization theory to the ambient health of the collective unconscious of Jungian psychology. We are also bypassing the literature on bureaucrat bashing to avoid casting discretionist schools as ill-tempered reaction formations.

2. Efficiency itself is a subsidiary ethical norm in utilitarianism. It relies on the validity of the rest of the construct for its own validation as means.

3. Rohr is certainly right to complain in the 1993 *PAR* symposium on this matter that Spicer and Terry have misread him. It is not the character of the particular founders that is at issue. They are but a conduit to a higher Truth. He is, as they are, looking for a certain underlying, or rather, superordinate calculus. This calculus is not the logic of formalized self-interest à la Buchanan and Tullock (1962), but the *telos* of a *polis*; the appropriate arrangements for the development of *virtu*.

4. Although this interpretation is well grounded in Rohr's texts, we must confess to a little exegesis ourselves. This is an unauthorized interpretation.

5. Despite their professed reliance on constitutionalism, much of the manifesto could be salvaged if they would abandon it. Goodsell's case for the public interest, that part of the agency perspective that is not wedded to institutions as given, and White's discourse on authority not only can stand alone, but, in our opinion, would be improved if they did (both essays in Wamsley et al., 1990).

3 The Growing Gap Between Words and Deeds

Postmodern Symbolic Politics

The first two sections of the previous chapter may be seen as a rather straight-forward aggregation of the standard arguments used to debunk the myth of U.S. representative democracy. To rehearse: The sovereign people express their will through the democratic accountability feedback loop, which is elaborated through rules and enforced through the chain of command. If the critique of that model were not enough to justify the need for a new middle-range normative theory of democratic possibilities in the United States, we now want to augment the critique by way of a safari through the jungle of postmodern thought. We will attempt both to describe postmodern conditions and to garner what we can from postmodern thought, which is both an explication of such conditions and an expression of postmodernism. The effects of this chapter, if valid, make loop strategies of reviving overhead democracy, constitutionalist schemes of ground-ing agency in the founding, and communitarian solutions based on citizen involvement implausible on grounds not covered in the previous chapter. As otherwise conceived, liberal democracy requires centered individuals, capable of autonomous will formation. Will formation, in turn, rests on intersubjective agreement about "reality." Postmodernism raises the possibility that such agree-ment about the "real" is now so ephemeral that it is incapable of founding informed policy discourse.

The distinction modern/postmodern is not likely to be a salient one for readers of the literature in which this book interposes itself. We press for it because it highlights aspects of advanced capitalist societies in which our discourse theory will have to win a place for itself. If the postmodern hypothesis is even partially valid—and only *partially* valid is what we believe it to be—two seemingly contradictory results may be deduced. First, there is no stable common "reality" against which truth claims may be redeemed. Instead, America today shares across disparate groups and tribes only a media-infused hyperreality of consciousness. This "reality" is transient and unstable and mutates rapidly. It is, as we will try to demonstrate, thin. Concomitantly, second, there is a refracted, more intimate, but perhaps incommensurable series of realities constructed by multiple subcultural fragments (Calinescu, 1991; Jameson, 1991). Governance, will formation, problem solving, citizen participation, and constitutional foundationalism are all rendered problematic under postmodern conditions. Our journey through postmodernism can be divided into five legs:

1. Signs, the symbols through which the public conversation is communicated, have become self-referential and epiphenomenal (i.e., derivative or second-order).
2. The accompanying danger is that diverse subcultures talk past one another (i.e., language games are incommensurable).
3. The political implications of hyperreality—a rapid sequence of images and symbols with unknown or uncertain referents racing through the public consciousness—are that simulation and media spectacle displace political debate.
4. The continuous struggle for meaning capture implies that symbolic politics, largely divorced from material distribution of valuables, matters most.
5. The concluding section assesses the effects of postmodernity on orthodoxy and its constitutionalist and communitarian competitors.

The voyage through these five waypoints will be prefaced forthwith by a brief description of the distinction modern/postmodern.

I. Modern/Postmodern

To utter *postmodern* is to imply a periodization, a division into eras. Such division, in turn, would seem to entail the intellectual obligation to explicate the underlying dynamics, historical tendencies, and organizational imperatives which distinguish one era from another. Most writers involved in the "postmodern turn" reject that task on the principle that such theorizing smacks precisely of the modernity they seek to transcend. We are not so principled. At the risk of vulgarizing postmodernity by using modernist precision, it can be proximately defined and situated, especially against the backdrop of the full flowering of modernism (i.e., high modernism).[1]

Assuming for the present chapter that one can take a standpoint within postmodernity and look back on modernity, it was that period from roughly the Enlightenment (the 18th century, with traces back to Descartes) at least through the 1950s. Modernity has considerable inertial force, propelling its canonical principles into and through the last half of the 20th century. To be sure, such landmarks do not hermetically seal off one era from another; neither individuals nor populations and their habits are suddenly reborn on some fixed date.

Modernity was well described by those with sociological imagination, like Weber, who lived within it. As a "structuration" (Giddens, 1984) or institutionalized cognition (an *episteme*), modernity was buttressed by a triumphant instrumental rationality set through science to the tasks of dominating and controlling all aspects of nature and life. Ambitious and arrogant, modern paradigm structurations are largely self-validating. As Jean-François Lyotard (1984) put it: "I will use the term modern to designate any science that legitimates itself with reference to a metadiscourse . . . [that makes] explicit appeal to some grand narrative" (p. xxiii). In other words, modern systems assume for themselves potentially an all-encompassing God's-eye, or Archimedean standpoint, under which all can be rendered amenable to that system or metanarrative (Calinescu, 1991; Rorty, 1979). Another way of putting it is that there is in modern thought an indefatigable urge to monism accompanied by the sin of reductionism. Examples of such metanarratives include logical positivism in philosophy of science, the canons of analytical logic in philosophy, the materialist dialectic in Marxism, and structural functionalism and systems theory in anthropology, sociology, and political science. In the field/problematic of public administration, the orthodox model discussed in Chapter 2 was the attempt of that discipline at constructing (imposing on lived experience) a metanarrative. Examples of the impulse to reductionism include: the one best way (Taylor), the basic element of life (DNA), the irreducible element of physics (quarks), the basic principle of reason (instrumental), the basic structure of truth justification (hypothesis testing), and the basic motivation of humans (self-interest).

Postmodern thinkers date back to Nietzsche (1844-1900), who told us God is dead, and include, by our reckoning, such American pragmatists as John Dewey and now Richard Rorty, much of existential phenomenology, and most typically what is called poststructuralist French philosophy (Derrida, Lyotard, Foucault, Baudrillard, and others). They are united by their skepticism toward those typically modern claims to what used to be called universalism or essentialism but is now gathered up under *foundationalism* or *metanarratives*. In turn, the consequences of antifoundationalism cluster

TABLE 3.1 General Traits of Modern vs. Postmodern Culture

Problematic	Modern	Postmodern
Architecture	Functional, bauhaus	Eclectic, referential
Mode of production	Mass assembly, factory	Postindustrial, information
Organization	Weberian hierarchy	Adhocracy, devolution
Sociology	Nuclear family	Fragmented households
Philosophy of science	Logical positivism	Methodological anarchy, interpretivism, ideography
Philosophy	Search for universals	Antifoundationalism
Psychology	Integrated authentic self	Decentered self
Ethics	Utilitarian, deontological, syllogistic	Situational
Media	Print linearity	Video, montage, MTV, channel surfing

around certain other signature themes, as we will see below. Postmodernism is the return of and revenge of the different, the assertion of the random nonpattern and the unassimilable anomaly. At risk, as the monolith fractures and then is deconstructed, is the loss of what western society took to be reality. If our ontological moorings are anchored in loose gravel, what price will we pay for the lack of putatively stable referents? One is reminded of Burke's vehement objection that the destruction of prejudices and myths by the then-rampaging analytic spirit of the French Revolution would rend the fabric of society. Now the analytic spirit is threatened with similar rupture.

As it has been iterated in various fields, the list of general traits in Table 3.1 is offered for the sake of making connection with heterogeneously educated readers. These oppositions share what might be called the entropic principle; differences between modern and postmodern may be variously expressed as:

integration versus disintegration
centralization versus decentralization
centripetal versus centrifugal
totalization versus fragmentation
metanarratives versus disparate texts
melting pot versus salad
commensurable versus incommensurable
the impulse to unify versus hyperpluralism
universalism versus relativism
Newton versus Heisenberg

Like the distinction art historians make between classical and romantic painting, music, and architecture, these bifurcations lack precision and should not be seen as hermetically sealed logician's categories (a and not-a); they are tendency statements.[2]

The next three sections explore postmodern conditions. We adduce evidence of, and the political prospects of, a world without anchor, cultures without stable referents, decentered selves without identities from which to speak or gesture.

II. Unstable Signs Leading to a Virtual Reality

The important effect of postmodern conditions, from the vantage point of political science and public administration, is that they hobble government and render useless national policy making in any sense of national interest. We are in danger of developing a politics of simulation or virtual reality, useful as a spectacle or entertaining diversion but not much help with the problems of governance. In the remainder of the chapter, we will explicate this problematic using the postmodern voice, a standpoint that provides the clearest possible rendering of what we mean by simulated politics.

A. STABLE COMMUNICATION/EPIPHENOMENALISM

The point we want to make in this section is that words, signs, and symbols, have become increasingly divorced from "reality." This is what we mean by *epiphenomenalism*. Words, signs, and symbols are increasingly unlikely to mean anything solid or lasting. Postmodern theory gives interpretive depth to these asocial aspects of language. We are rendered speechless by such tendencies as media-induced consumerism, negative political advertisements, and sound-bite and photo-op political journalism. We want to report and sort these insights from postmodernist thinking. But first, in order to assess the radical epiphenomenalism of signs, a base by which their distance from referents may be so judged is required.

This section is not offered as a careful argument of semiotics or epistemology, but rather is similar in purpose to Baudrillard's (1983, pp. 11ff.) speculations or Jameson's (1991, p. 96) use of *imaginary* to express a similar point. Sustained rigorous arguments that are compatible include Habermas (1972, see especially chap. 5) and Wittgenstein (1953). Baudrillard (1981,

p. 158ff.), on whom we shall rely for insights into postmodern epiphenomenalism, denies even this much reality to signs. It should also be noted that by beginning with human linguistic communication, we have assumed away the philosophical dualism that attributes reality only to physical/material noumenal objects. We assume in advance, in other words, a position congruent with Berger and Luckmann's (1966) "social construction of reality."

Subsection 1, on denotation/connotation, proposes a genealogy of language which provides a minimally unassailable ground of authentic communication. Subsection 2, on reality/hyperreality, explores the stability of modernist metanarratives, against which postmodern signs seem spectral and haunting. Subsection 3, on production/information, offers both political-economic evolutions and philosophical turns as being influential in the thinning of "reality."

1. Denotation/Connotation

Suppose that the origins of language consisted of comic-strip cave persons (like Peter and Thor in the comic strip B.C.) gesturing with variable grunts to objects in their environment essential to their survival: Snake, piece of heavy wood, rock, goat, cave. Such signs are called denotative; they denote particular singular objects. Denotative signs were long thought by such schools of philosophy as logical positivism (Carnap, 1959a, 1959b; Neurath, 1959) and British empiricism to be the essential building blocks of communication and science. Language, by this view, was anchored by direct one-to-one picture representations of objects. Although this view lives on in the unexamined assumptions of sophomoric science, it is no longer hegemonic in philosophy or semiotics. Wittgenstein (1953) has taught us that strictly denotative signs are not the paradigmatic cornerstone of communication. Denotative signs occur in language games predicated on cooperative action. Denotative signs have, when uttered, already connotative implications, which depend on the context in which they are used. Thus snake = possibly dangerous and venomous attacker or lunch, piece of heavy wood = weapon or tool, rock = tool, place to sit, or something to throw, goat = thing to eat or milk, cave = sheltered hiding place. The denotative- connotative continuum implies face-to-face communication in a common sensual milieu, and it enables social action. Watch out! Let's drink from the waters. Sleep in cave at peace. Stalk, surround, kill, and share goat meat.[3] The connotative gathers up the denotative and provides the purposeful reason for its employment.

2. Reality/Hyperreality

The ability of humans to use signs under modalities of cooperation, however, carries with it the transcendent talent of abstraction and use of metaphors. Humans also enjoy using startling oppositions, provoking laughter. With a memory capable of mixed scanning and categorical sorting, along with the playful capacity to exaggerate, mimic, lie, and act out (dogs, for instance, cannot feign excitement), the human talent for communication leads not only to storytelling, but also to theory, philosophy, and religion (what Marxists call superstructure). These cultural creations are manifested in reification, hypostatization (construing a conceptual entity as a real existent), alienation, and schizophrenia.[4] These manifestations of communicative culture share a tendency to outrace or transcend the denotative-connotative continuum from which their original elements were derived. The abstraction, be it a category, a story, or an entire religion, is objectified or "thingified"; a hegemonic reality is attributed to it. As with Platonic forms, a hidden but more profound reality is thought to be behind the "mere" appearances gathered up by the denotative-connotative continuum. A paradigmatic example comes from Feuerbach's (1881) critique of religious alienation. Using the so-called transformative method, he explicated the move of human thought from the denotative-connotative continuum (e.g., humans can exercise power over their environment) to the projection of this thought onto a humanly created abstraction (God is all powerful and makes "man" in His image). This abstraction was then interpreted as dominating humans (God forbids sins). Thus God is alienated man (Avineri, 1968, pp. 11-12). Man made God in his own image and then vested the abstraction with powers over man.

The history of civilization is filled with incidents of abstract thought racing beyond everyday life to confuse and overwhelm its denotative-connotative gestures. Religious wars may be counted among the instances where abstractions ascend over lifeworld discourse. Although abstract thought of any kind may be regarded as just that—abstract and with problematical relation to the denotative-connotative continuum of authentic everyday lived communication—abstractions may also be categorized as having more or less density and fixity. We are leading up to the generalization that postmodern reifications have less of such density and fixity.

Premodern and modern thought, however fundamentally misleading their metadiscourse pretensions may now be judged, had higher density than postmodern ones, if only because of their longevity as categories fixed in the minds, and reproduced in the activities, of successive generations. The concepts of civilization, divine right of kings, or sovereignty may not have had exact experiential referents, but they were considerably more stable, slower-moving targets than are the constructs of postmodernity. Modern constructs may point to nothing "real"; they might be distortions or idealizations of "reality." But they were not ephemeral in the same sense as is postmodernists' hyperreality. Those modern, big ideas did not flit across consciousness for a moment, only to disappear and be replaced by others. Because of their longevity, complexity, and density, modern metanarratives, or paradigms, or *Weltanschauungen,* or epistemes were capable of *truth functionality.* That is to say, within these systems, one could show contradiction, have disputations amenable to resolution, make claims, and demand that they be "discursively redeemable." For elites with leisure to engage in such pursuits, the density of the metanarrative was sufficient to comfort them that a hold on something "real" was possible.

3. Production/Information

We have pointed to a denotative-connotative linguistic base of human "reality." We have argued that a superstructure of self-justifying metanarratives was once sufficiently stable to give the appearance of "reality." Both forms of *real* are increasingly problematic in the postmodern condition.

As long as most humans were forced to earn their living by producing commodities in groups, as was the case through modernity, a sufficiently robust linguistic base of denotative-connotative communicative speech acts would refer to the "real" commodities planted and harvested, crafted, or rolled off the assembly line. And authentic, sincere communication would be required for the cooperative acts needed to produce them. In the realm of civil society, relatively stable family units, neighborhoods, and religious communities would also assure sufficient human interaction to provide a bedrock of authentic denotative-connotative mutuality. The thesis of Jean Baudrillard (1981, chap. 2)—corresponding to insights from sociologists such as Daniel Bell, communication theorists such as Marshall McLuhan, and neo-Marxist political economy (see Kellner, 1989; Poster, 1990)—is that this robust base is lost when advanced industrial societies move from an emphasis on production to an emphasis on consumption and information. As fewer and fewer people earned their living by growing, mining, and manufacturing commodities, as machines and electrification replaced brute human labor, and now as more and more people earn their vouchers to consume by manipulating information and symbols (often persuading others to consume), the viscosity of "reality" thins. This thinning is exacerbated by the exponential multiplication of advertising messages that inundate consumers, informing them that consumption is now vastly more important than production. There is, then, a direct connection between postindustrial society and the postmodern condition.

The concomitant thinning of superstructural metanarratives has been the main work of philosophy in the last half of the 20th century. As Rome was battered and finally destroyed by successive waves of barbarians, so has the foundationalist/modern metanarrative canon been battered by Nietzsche, pragmatists, existentialists, phenomenologists, semioticians, poststructuralists, deconstructionists, hermeneuticists, and more. Nietzsche's dictum that God is dead is now being spread to all God's-eye perspectives. All the metanarratives of science, metaphysics, and epistemology are being mercilessly deconstructed with the same tools used against reasoned defenses of religion. Reason and science, having triumphed over myths and superstitions, have turned back in on themselves and have eroded their own bases of confident assertion.

B. REFERENTS YIELD TO SELF-REFERENTIAL SIGNS

Denotative-connotative signs occur within stable language games of modernity where truth was an observable or at least debatable matter. Postmodern epiphenomenal signs rely more on each other (i.e., they are *self-referential*) and begin to float away from any "real" referents (making them epiphenomenal). Jameson (1991) has called this the "free and random play of signifiers" (p. 96). Baudrillard (1983) goes so far as to claim that nonreferential signs take charge (sort of a semiotic hegemony) and determine "the real." The change from a production economy to one centered on consumption, along with the recent battering of modernist metanarratives by intellectual critique, provides the historical conditions for this postmodern hyperreality. The task remains to describe these conditions. Ferreting out all the subtleties of postmodern hyperreality is beyond our capacity,[5] but the dynamic pattern by which signs become self-referential seems clear enough. The following moments each require explication:

1. The spread of monologic "commun"-ication,
2. leading to the creation of pseudocommunities,
3. allowing the free-play signifiers to become self-referential, and
4. the return of self-referential logos to influence perception in the lifeworld.

1. Monologic Communication

If one accepts the proposition that "reality" is a social construction or structuration, it follows that intersubjective interaction and communication generate this social construction of reality. An intersubjective reality would have a certain agonistic quality stemming from the heterogeneity of those whose acts, words, and gazes hold the community together. Active participants sustain their reality via a denotative-connotative language game where there is a verbal struggle over both the denotation and the connotation of signs.

That kind of intersubjective social communication is disrupted in conditions of postmodernity, and the roots of the disruption may be traced to modernist practices. Hummel (1994) identifies a monologic form of communication and links it to bureaucratized language, in which the world of robust social action is displaced by the world of rationally organized, bureaucratic action. Obedience to hierarchically commanded routines supersedes empathic relationships with clients; savvy clients who regularly interact with functionaries learn to separate meaning from the message. And in bureaucracy, because language is separated from the intentions of the speaker, the individual functionary need not be personally committed to his or her words. To blame the functionary for official utterances is to mistake one-dimensional monologue for robust social conversation. One does not have authentic conversations with bureaucratized functionaries; no problem solving or social sense making will occur because the problem has been preidentified and its solution already put into place (Hummel, 1994). There is no dialogue, no opportunity to express the agonistic tension, no opportunity to engage in a verbal struggle to define a problem and decide what should be done about it. This arrest of agonistic tension characterizes postmodern language games.

Agonistic tension is lost when instead of *communal or dialogical* communication, the dominant mode of message transfer is *monologic*. The first moment of this dialectic is the separation and transforming of the role of speaker/listener into two roles. The next moment begins with the increasing ubiquity and hegemony of one-way utterances, unchecked by the possibility of immediate retort. Hence the communal dialogue devolves into a monologue. A paradigm case is the rise and spread of broadcast media.[6] Although the proliferation of monologic broadcast media messages corresponds to, and is a signature of, the postmodern condition, we would caution against any leaps to the deterministic logic of cause and effect (as in "TV caused the postmodern condition"), but TV represents a case in point.

The deduction that broadcast media are monologic requires little demonstration. Obviously, most viewers and listeners cannot talk back.[7] There is virtually no communicative reciprocity, no dialogue. One can only switch channels or turn off the set. On behalf of "broadcast central," affirmation is measured in Nielsen-type ratings, market share, and the viewer purchase of advertised products. But even here an atomistic individual is only marginally empowered to affirm or negate—he or she may purchase the same product anyway, with or without having watched the TV show. What an individual personally watches or turns off is very unlikely to be charted. The monologue needs the participation of no one in particular. Response is diffuse.

2. Pseudocommunities

Monologic community alters radically the notion of community. The term *broadcast*, for example, implies casting from some central location to an unspecified, dispersed audience of receivers. An epiphenomenal message sent from a central location can be received by millions of viewers and auditors. The sound bite and image goes forth and creates a chaotic, constantly shifting pseudocommunity momentarily brought together only by that message. This pseudocommunity need not share class position, worksite, age, gender, geographic area, or ideological predisposition. The pseudocommunity changes actual membership each nanosecond, even while being constant in a statistical sense. At the receiving end of the encoding-decoding communication sequence are vastly varied levels of attention and engagement—from the passive, dazed, half-drunk couch potato to the channel-surfing stimulation glutton (expressing two responses to boredom). The participation that does occur is very much controlled and allowed only on terms set by broadcast central: send money to the televangelist to continue the mission; see your pledge registered on the big board; call in to Larry King or Phil Donahue; compete for a place on the game show; vacation in Hollywood and be part of a "live" audience.

3. Self-Referencing and Simulacra

Without lifeworld community, TV communication is more or less self-contained and is thus self-referential. On TV, history is a rerun of the TV programs shown during the Kennedy administration, or a 30-second spot about the "historic Ice Bowl" football game. The more a language/practice is removed from the face-to-face context of a daily life, where social relationships are

reproduced through dialogue, the more language must generate and reproduce those features from within itself. Media-created, postmodern, epiphenomenal language must simulate its context and ventriloquize its audience.
Because there is no clearly determinate referential world outside the broadcast
to provide a standard against which to evaluate the flow of meanings, subjects
have no defined identity as players in the conversation. When that is the case
(i.e., no constraining resistance of an alternatively constitutive ontological base),
"the real" is only self-referentially so (Poster, 1990, p. 45).

The concept of *simulacra* illustrates self-referentiality. Because receivers
do not communicate back, TV communication traffics in simulacra: endless
proliferation of copies for which no original actually exists (Jameson, 1991,
p. 18). The career of Mr. T, who originally appeared in the TV series *The
A-Team,* provides a convenient example. The character was a gruff, outland-
ishly clothed, iron pumping, good-hearted, black, tough Vietnam veteran; a
composite—somewhat ridiculous but positive—copy of no "real" individual
original. He was a metaphor and a simulacrum. The character was then made
into a Saturday cartoon series referring back to the series: a simulacrum of
a simulacrum. Similarly, anchormen, those beefcake teleprompter readers
seen on TV, are sent to exotic locales dressed up in safari jackets with chest
hair peeking out to become simulacra of (now defunct) on-the-scene report-
ers in possession of hard-won situational understanding of the events they
are covering. Then, in the stream-of-consciousness entailed by the mixing
of "hard news" with messages from sponsors, make-believe anchors (hardly
distinguishable from "real" anchors) deliver the fast-breaking news on
brand-name coffee or weight-loss programs: simulacra of simulacra.

Programming may also be seen as self-referential in the sense of complying
with a master template etched by the imperatives of clock time. The length of
programming and consequently its level of generalization is not, like primordial
language games or even books, substantively driven. They are arranged
according to clock time to regularize the selling of commercial slots. The
amount of time to be filled is given and determining. The plots of sitcoms or
detective cop shows are driven by the rhythm of commercial breaks and conflict
resolution on the half-hour or hour. Minute changes in diffuse audience preferences doom one series while vaulting to fame the virtually interchangeable stars
of other almost-identical ones. In a Freudian sense, the *eros* evoked by beautiful
stars is canceled out by the *thanatos* of endless repetition.

But it is in news broadcasting—putatively the reflection of the "real" upon
which public policy might be based—that self-referential hyperreality is
most apparent. The distinction between news and entertainment is increas-

ingly permeable (e.g., *Murphy Brown* became political fodder, Pee Wee Herman made news, *The Today Show* is a news-entertainment-educational-commercial promo melange). Curiously, one doesn't get different news from different networks. From an almost infinite number of potential events that could become news, virtually the same events will be reported in the 22 minutes allowed by each network for the news. News is not so much what happens as what gets reported. In this sense the news is created by the media from ambient lifeworld happenings. Once an event or persona has been thus vaulted to the realm of media happening, he, she, or it is vested with newsworthiness and becomes part of hyperreality. Multiple repetitions of an event, such as the beating of Rodney King by Los Angeles police officers, reverberate for days, weeks, months, and years as the preface to reporting the latest developments. Once part of hyperreality, they are analyzed by talking heads, become metaphors to shape perception of other events (all scandals are "-gates"), arc reprised at year-end as one of the top 10 stories, and are historicized by recall at every anniversary divisible by 10.

Again, as hyperreality has no anchor in dialogic discourse, no check outside itself, the dynamic of it favors increasing shrillness, vulgarity, shock value depictions of violence, bizarre human relationships (e.g., *Geraldo* topics might include outed cross-dressing skinheads), and ever more provocative and insulting talk show hosts. From the moment one gets up at the urging of the clock radio, through breakfast with Bryant and Katie, and including traffic updates and happy talk during long commutes, to prime-time TV at night, one is inundated by hundreds of messages. Naturally, broadcasters are motivated to shrillness to ensure that their voices pierce through what the postmodern consciousness might otherwise take as part of background white noise. As shrillness intensifies, media-infused hyperreality is increasingly distanced from denotative-connotative language discourse. This hyperreality would disintegrate in modern conditions, where challenges could be offered and claims could be judged against agreed-upon standards. But in postmodern conditions standards are seen as arbitrary and, moreover, behavior is influenced by this hyperreality. For example, a plausible hypothesis is that gun violence, macho sexual behavior, and homicide—first depicted on TV for their entertainment/market value—influence behavior in postmodern conditions.[8]

4. The Return of Self-Referential Logos: The Coding of the Real

To qualify as a dialectic relationship, a matter must exhibit circular causality with cumulative effect (Ollman, 1971, p. 58). The semiotic dialectic we have sketched begins with agonistic dialogue, a language game of modernity, but then disintegrates. From there it moves through the overdevelopment of a monologic pole and becomes one-way communication. Concomitant to the monologue is the creation of pseudocommunities insufficiently robust to check the free play of signifiers. Hence communication becomes self-referential. But to what effect on public policy and public administration? Let us investigate the matter by assuming the worst and later hold out hope that humans are capable of learning their way out of the predicament we describe.

Baudrillard (1983) is the most deterministic of postmodern thinkers. To him the hyperreal of self-referential signs replaces whatever might have been "real" and determines it. Although not closely reasoned, the argument seems to be that a self-referential sign may be seen as a logo. As conceptualized by Jameson (1991):

> A logo is something like the synthesis of an advertising image and a brand name; better still, it is a brand name which has been transformed into an image, a sign or emblem which carries the memory of a whole tradition of earlier advertisements within itself in a well-nigh intertextual way. (p. 85)

Does seeing the golden arches on the freeway cause one's children to salivate? Logos, in turn, may be seen as species of codes. Codes are defined as provisional and shifting rules by which hyperreality shapes lifeworld perceptions and hence experiences. The logo Nike, for instance, is an intertextual montage of images and slogans (sweating, svelte, and muscular bodies, Michael Jordan, "just do it") which in addition to selling overdesigned shoes and pricey sportswear, acts as a code such that these images attach themselves also to those buying and wearing the logo. Thus Nike codes someone as committed to fitness and probably also a desirable sexual partner. This imagery is perhaps called forth by the logo prominently displayed on a T-shirt. Pop novelists may write that "she was a Birkenstock girl," conjuring up the image of a youngish, stringy-haired, unreconstructed hippie who has remained true to the zeitgeist of 1969. A recent automobile campaign emphasized codes to the extent that the car itself was not shown. Buy yourself a Stetson, some pointy-toed high-heeled boots, some "classic" blue jeans, and a gaudy belt buckle, and you too can cast yourself in the Wild West simulacrum.

The plausibility of codes (whether or not they are designed as logos) determining or influencing perception, experience, and attitudes was brought to our attention by the example of friends who are residents of relatively secure suburban middle-class enclaves. They live in fear of drive-by shootings, gang violence, and car-jackings, not because they or anyone close to them has experienced these threats directly but because the media, with a 20 million-person experiential base, reports them nightly. One's own secure existence is less "real" than the "reality" of the nightly news and film at 11. One's own frozen water pipes, a fire, or running off the road in the fog is not "real" unless affirmed by airtime on the nightly news. One's family misfortunes are not "real" unless simulated on *Picket Fences, People's Court,* or (no one should be so unlucky) *Geraldo,* where epiphenomena have displaced experience. Hard-working middle-class African American males complain that others give them wide berth, avoid eye contact, will even cross to the other side of the street when approaching. The encounter is precoded, often not by phenomenological experience but by experience of the epiphenomenal. So there seems to be some extent to which hyperreality comes back around to influence perception, experience, and attitudes.

C. THE THINNING OF "REALITY"

Section A established modernity as a ground of relatively stable communication and then ascertained the historical conditions of its erosion, setting the stage for the epiphenomenal signifiers. Section B explicated a dialectical pattern (exemplified by broadcast media) whereby signs become self-referential. We now turn to the question: how pervasive is the thinning of "reality"? Or, less ambitiously, what other signatures of the dialectic of self-referential signs may be adduced? Let's take an airplane trip, go to a theme park, and experience a war.

1. Monological Experiences in Serialized Communities

As we have argued, modernity possessed shared standards from which truth functions could be derived. Modernity had totalitarian tendencies, but we could in common assess the truth of such claims as "the trains run on time." We knew what trains were, we had timetables to tell us what "on time" meant, and we had clocks that reported time. Now the claim that planes run on time can only be assessed by a statistical artifact developed by airlines to prove that they do. Worse, this statistical artifact is believably delivered to us by our surrogate sister or brother, the flight attendant, in ways that invite neither questioning nor dissent. Likewise, passengers herded and cramped into a disabled, stuffy, crowded plane parked on the Tarmac are thanked for the patience they neither felt nor expressed. Authentic dialogue and information dissemination are possible, but passengers are instead treated like media consumers and their response is ventriloquized. Passengers, perhaps conditioned to silent acquiescence to what is broadcast, do not demand the precise meaning of "short delay." Announcements are monologic. Passengers, as undifferentiated ciphers, are a pseudocommunity thrown together by random forces. They are what Sartre (Hirsh, 1981, p. 76ff.) would call a serialized group, a series of otherwise atomized individuals brought together only by the coincidence of an airplane schedule. Atomized, they have none of the solidarity of an authentic community through which they might demand better treatment and more human mutuality.

Vacations, too, are spent consuming monologues in serialized pseudocommunities, especially at theme parks. Long queues are artfully designed to give the appearance of progress toward the attraction; young interchangeable guides spiel humorous patois by rote to acquiescent individuals and families thrown together by chance. Photos of the simulated good time, suitable for framing, may be purchased at the conclusion. If not, helpful signs erected by Kodak (logo) will tell one where to snap to preserve the memory of what never was. And, wherever one goes, one arrives at a destination in which the milieu is almost the same as the one just left: same airport, same restaurants, same freeways leading to the same mall. Populating these facade simulacra are interchangeable people, ciphers with the corporate uniform, logo, and smile. The many actors fitting themselves into Mickey Mouse suits in Disney theme parks in California, Florida, Tokyo, France, and now Virginia become simulacra of an imaginary mouse. History itself becomes commodified simulacra: Colonial Williamsburg with its (oxymoronic) "authentic reproductions"; the movie set for the epic film *Alamo* (more popular than the real [i.e., authentically reproduced] one); jam-packed ghost towns with shootouts on the hour (see Huxtable, 1992). And coming soon for your enjoyment is interactive virtual reality from within a wired helmet.

2. Can the Real Be Distinguished From the Virtual?

Can postmodern humans sustain the critical ability to differentiate between simulated history and "reality," on the one hand, and more authentic phenomenological experience of the lifeworld, on the other? After all, even war seems epiphenomenal, like a TV miniseries followed by parades. But a miniseries would seem more "real" than the way the Gulf War was experienced.

One saw journalists breathlessly groping for their gas masks, ambiguous pictures of greenish fireworks incoherently interpreted (by journalists). Then "public information" officers (journalists in uniform) briefed civilian journalists; and then journalists interviewed retired military experts (now employed as journalists); then journalists talked to other journalists about the plight of journalists in hotels (Bernie was under the table, suicidal Peter was looking out the window). Then journalists analyzed the role of journalism in modern warfare. The message is the self-referential media. With rare exception, coverage took place without benefit of firsthand accounts (and even these were suspect; one firsthand account turned out to be false testimony from a Kuwaiti diplomat's daughter, a media event arranged by a Washington consulting firm). In war—expressed as self-referential epiphenomenalism— there are no burned bodies, no bloody corpses being tossed up on the back of a truck. Instead, journalists talk to journalists, thus unleashing an endless cascade of symbols or names for putative events which no "viewer" has in fact experienced. Immediate reports on Patriot Missile kill ratios seem, on later analysis, to have been greatly overestimated—the green flashes one saw over Saudi Arabia, or rather, on CNN, were not indicators of successful interceptions of incoming Scud missiles. By late 1993, journalists began deflating the wondrous technology balloon that they had earlier inflated.[9]

The epiphenomenal character of the Gulf War may explain its short-lived political effects. Memories of more densely experienced wars were long-lasting, and their political effects rippled out for generations. Republican strategists for Bush must have shaken their heads in wonderment at the fleeting euphoria of Gulf War victory and high approval rates in the polls, alongside the subsequent free fall in the electoral prospects of the incumbent. His decline was eclipsed the next year by the once-popular Canadian Prime Minister Kim Campbell's electoral loss in which her majority Progressive-Conservative Party was reduced to two seats. Seemingly almost at random, kaleidoscopic shifts in the postmodern hyperreality can popularize a president or prime minister one year, and defeat the same person in the polls in a later year. A plausible hypothesis is that such social amnesia is the result of the thin viscosity of media-infused postmodern hyperreality. Those who live by the image. . . .

We will consider again the political effects of postmodern hyperreality later. Our immediate purpose has been to attribute at least marginal validity to the proposition that modern "reality" has evolved to postmodern hyperreality. One way to sum up is to recall early Enlightenment/Modern philosopher Descartes's famous rationalist premise: "I think, therefore I am."

Subsequently, Marx thought: "I labor productively, therefore I am." Now "I shop, therefore I am" seems to be more resonant. That is to say, we are not as inner-directed as consumers as we were as thinkers or producers. Those earlier identities-through-creative-activity were not as susceptible to symbolic manipulation as the later postmodern identities; they produced more centered selves. Thinkers and producers had an autonomous base of personal experience not so easily dislodged and set loose by the symbol makers; they had a firmer grasp of their own creations.

III. Neotribalism and the Decentered Self

At a level of abstraction worthy of Hegel, Spengler, and Toynbee, the demise of a hegemonic entity results in centripetal fragmentation. The lifting of the smothering weight of Soviet communism, for instance, releases previously pent-up nationalist identities and aspirations. Earlier, the demise of the Austria-Hungarian empire resulted in Balkanization. Postmodern theory posits a similar dialectic whereby the withering of hegemonic modernism leads to refracted postmodernism. Specifically, when what is perceived in common across classes, genders, and regions as "reality" is self-referential and vacuous, what is called forth and allowed to germinate is diverse worldviews of previously oppressed subcultures. And these worldviews, such as Serbian nationalism, are already nascently complete, now freed to express their holographic visions and particular interpretations unimpeded by the resistance heretofore afforded by a universalistic hegemonic worldview. At the macrolevel reality is thin. At microlevels thick interpretations of "reality" fill the legitimacy vacuum. Queer Nation, religious denominations, Branch Davidians, Black Nationalists, Aryan Nation, Crips, and other groups step forth with self-referencing paradigms that members can be taught. Put another way, the thinness of the putatively dominant, shared culture calls forth a plurality of thick, robust, self-contained communities, the borders of which are watchfully guarded by their leaders and intellectuals. The crucial question is whether this plurality of views is a new tribalism, prelude to a tower of babel, or a precondition for an enriched discourse freed from the fetters of the monolithic modern canon. The cogency of the contrary tribalism thesis we present next rests on three interrelated themes of postmodern thought: (a) otherness and difference, (b) incommensurability between others, and (c) the decentered self.

A. OTHERNESS AND INCOMMENSURABILITY

Postmodernism, as a mode of thought or point of view (rather than the historic era which we have called postmodernity), is a celebration and legitimization of "otherness" and "difference." This follows from its attack on modern foundationalism and its decimation of metanarratives. Again, the demise of universal metanarratives puts previously stable meanings in play; they are up for grabs. Feminists and other groups of others, those who embody difference, claim quite logically that the now-discredited universality of the canons of the Enlightenment were but the special pleadings of white, propertied, patriarchal, Eurocentric privileged classes. More telling, a kind of affirmative action of worldviews is pressed. Other, different ways of being and ways of seeing merit heightened respect because of past suppression by those (what we now know as) partial but canonically arrogant worldviews. In postmodern conditions, any special pleading has equal claim to validity. Moreover, other different ways of being and ways of seeing merit extra consideration because of past suppression under the influence of the dominant metanarrative, now viewed as illegitimately dominant. Hence Zurab Tsereteli's 311-foot statue of the great sea captain Christopher Columbus, intended as a goodwill gift from Russia on the 500th anniversary of his voyage to San Salvador, goes begging for a home, its head in Fort Lauderdale and the other pieces, last we heard, still in St. Petersburg, Russia. "Others" have judged Columbus guilty of genocide and exploitation and are unwilling any longer to be victims of the hegemony in which they are other.

But if all pleadings are special, why would any individual situated in one subcultural fragment with its particular worldview bother to assess the validity of different ones? If one's otherness and difference are to be celebrated, it follows that precisely those aspects of an identity that are radically other would be accentuated while similarities would be downplayed or ignored. The proliferation of othernesses means that social fragmentation persists and distends.

The plurality of thick paradigms of subcultures, enabled by the depthlessness of common culture and illegitimacy of high culture, raises the specter of incommensurability (see Bernstein, 1992, chap. 3, for accessible explication). Attention to the problem of incommensurability, as a matter of intellectual history, has been largely the result of Kuhn's (1970) best-seller, *The Structure of Scientific Revolutions.* Kuhn argued that scientific paradigms are, in relation to one another, incommensurable. A paradigm is a system of logically interrelated propositions, the sum of which are taken to adequately explain phenomena in a given field of scientific inquiry. Paradigms become threatened when phenomena do not behave according to a paradigm's propositions; these phenomena are called anomalies. The proliferation of anomalous phenomena gives rise to competing theoretical systems that claim to better account for all phenomena previously explained, as well as the anomalies that have emerged. Science progresses, according to Kuhn, by the revolutionary vanquishing of an older paradigm by a newer one. Kuhn's history of science, however, indicated that the victory of one paradigm over another is less a matter of superior coherence and explanatory fecundity and more a matter of the replacement of an older generation of scholars by a younger one. Discussion, dialogue, and academic disputation do not settle issues because radically different presuppositions are not amenable to evidence or refutation; the presuppositions determine in advance what evidence is acceptable as refutation. One set of paradigmatic assumptions simply cannot "see" evidence and data thrown up by a different set.

If people talk past one another in science, the bastion of reason and exemplar of civil disputation, can we expect better from other cults? Can the Christian right be expected to give up basic life-validating presuppositions to work out agreements of toleration with flamboyant gays? If science operates by way of decidedly uncivil paradigmatic revolutions (not evolutions), can we expect better modes of conflict resolution between, say, skinheads and Crips? Can civility and transparadigmatic empathy be expected between those who believe they are victimized by Eurocentric cultural dominance and those whose life project has been precisely dedicated to the preservation and dissemination of Shakespeare, Milton, Plato, and the traditions which such figures express? Does one group have to die of old age to allow the fruition of otherness? Kuhn's work with hard science, where evidence might be more compelling and less subjective than in the above-mentioned disputations, suggests a disappointing answer to these questions. With nothing in common but hyperreality, individuals are ships passing in the night without running lights.

A less extreme example of fragmentation is close to home. Political science, in the lifetime of some of us, was once a discipline, a monistic world of commonality. It had a solid (now mythical) epistemological base in logical positivist philosophy of science. It had a set of methods called behavioralism, justified by that base. It had a shared problematic and typical queries presented to it from shared benign assumptions about the American polity (see democratic accountability feedback loop in Chapter 2). No matter what one's specialty was or was evolving toward, there were common landmark books, concepts, and hall-of-fame authors duly anointed to be presidents of the American Political Science Association. Only a very few legitimate journals were read by everyone, and publishing in them was the ticket to national recognition, prestige, and tenure. This would be a moment of high modernism for political science, lasting roughly the same 25 years as the American Century. We submit that political science is no longer a discipline in the sense just described. Its "reality" has thinned as its base was discredited, its methods challenged, its comfortable cognitions themselves made problematic both by events (e.g., Vietnam, Watergate, assassinations, voter apathy) and powerful intellectual criticism stemming from those events.

Political science is now an umbrella term, like a freeway turnoff sign leading to a mall filled with specialty shops, under which an increasingly fragmented series of groups meet. The proliferation of sections, similarly multiplied in all learned societies, is evidence of this. Separate journals have sprung up to accommodate diverse specialties, methodologies, and even ideologies. Under conditions of disciplinary fragmentation, it is scarcely possible to have a national hall-of-fame reputation like, say, Schattschneider, Truman, or V. O. Key. We now have national reputations among networks of approximately 80 similarly engaged scholars who have read, appreciate, and cite our work. We would guess that people from one group, say urban politics, rarely have serious substantive discussions with those from other groups, say international relations formal modelers. Members of different specialties do not read the same material, keep up with the same journals, or get excited by the same new landmark book. Indeed, it is not wise to be a generalist. One can have intense and detailed knowledge of no more than two sub-subfields to which one speaks and in which one is published. Is it not ironic that the only books we have in common are gimmicky, kitschy introductory American government texts designed for the truncated attention span of our postmodern students?[10]

To be sure, the development of disciplinary fractions is not necessarily evidence of insurmountable paradigmatic incompatibility of the type described by Kuhn. A more accurate label might be quasi-incommensurable. Separated, tribalized discourse communities can isolate themselves from one another by inattention and disdain, as much as by paradigmatic dissonance at a fundamental epistemological level. The more an individual's identity is connected to a subcultural fragment, the more is this identity replaced with more precise social formations—"urbanist" or "modeler" replaces "political scientist"; Branch Davidian replaces Christian; feminist or gay replaces middle-class American. Incommensurability and quasi-incommensurability seem to gain the upper hand. The potential result of neotribalism is that the micropolitics of identity affirmation replaces more generalized national and international will formation. As Jameson (1991) put it: "The stupendous proliferation of social codes today into professional and disciplinary jargons (but also into the badges of affirmation of ethnic, gender, race, religious, and class-factional adhesion) is also a political phenomenon, as the problem of micropolitics sufficiently demonstrates" (p. 17).

But can't we transcend such limitations of macroscopic vacuity and microscopic identity distillations? Not if decentered postmodernity speaks us.

B. THE DECENTERING OF THE SELF

Our democratic institutions, economic reward system, legal system, ethical schemes, and pedagogical traditions all have as cornerstone the tacit assumption of autonomous individual selves. An individual chooses freely and is responsible for the choices. Individuals have unique points of view that are the infinitely variable compilations of genetic endowment and historical-cultural life experience. This understanding of the self is under attack by virtually all of the *isms* collected under the rubric of postmodernism. Perhaps for shock value or because rhetorical overkill is also popular in philosophy, the death of the subject has been announced (Foucault, 1970). However varied the subsequent retheorizing of the self, postmodernism is united in disparaging the self of modernity and the Enlightenment as being "too centered, too unified, too rationalist, in short too Cartesian" (Poster, 1989, p. 53); the constituting self implied by the cogito ("I think, therefore I am") is an impossible ideal.

A strong, autonomous, constituting self stands in contradiction to the postmodern views that stress the uniqueness of language games or the social construction of reality. All such postmodern analyses coincide with malleable individuals. Pragmatists, for instance, posit a "mirror image self" whereby an individual is the current running sum of how others react to and regard that self. French poststructuralists emphasize the importance of the particular structure or *episteme,* the unquestioned, even totalitarian way of thinking and being which establishes behavioral expectations in all the interstices of life. Ingersoll and Adams (1992) documented such a dominant mode of thinking: the tacit organization. Baudrillard, as we have seen, goes so far as to proclaim that the vacuous, self-referential codes *speak us*: We are the Birkenstock girl, the Nike guy, or the urban cowboy. In the field of literary criticism, the authorial self, thought in the past to create literary texts, is now conceived as the expression of the larger text; the South speaks Faulkner.

What is important for our purposes is that decentered selves are insufficiently solid to resist either the thinning of reality or neotribalism.

IV. Postmodern Conditions:
Orthodoxy, Constitutionalism, and Communitarianism

The postmodern citizenry is not so much informed as bombarded with fleeting images designed mainly to manipulate consumers. Emblematic of the monologic communication that now characterizes the public conversation, TV yields up a hyperreality of commodities and symbols that only monied interests can afford to sustain. The barriers to these communications outlets are substantial; campaigns costing hundreds of thousands of dollars represent the minimum ante for a national issue or office.[11] The viscosity of "reality" thins as TV reality, the monologic tendency of postmodern communication, ascends. Postmodern politics is the simulated politics of symbol manipulation.

A. MODERN AND POSTMODERN SYMBOLIC POLITICS

To declare that elites manipulate symbols does not require postmodern critique; but the interaction between modernist symbol manipulations and postmodern simulated politics is worth investigating. Murray Edelman (1964, 1971, 1977, 1988), whose symbolic politics is grounded in modernity, has been the leading theorist of symbolic politics in political science. In the textbook replication-simplification of Edelman's work, symbolic politics assuages the less powerful while the rewards of material policy, the important stuff, abounds to the benefit of the influential, the organized, and, what makes these possible, the monied classes. By this analysis, the rhetorical preambles to legislative bills (e.g., save the family farm) are developed for unanalytical popular consumption. Obversely, the fine print and subclauses encompass the distributive policies benefiting agribusiness conglomerates. This was an analysis that fit the conditions of high modernity. And, however distorted in favor of organized interests, policy actually did build freeways, electrify the national outback, and construct the suburbs. With all its faults and skews, it was "real" government. Orthodoxy may have needed reform, but it had legitimacy and truth value. That has changed.

1. Symbolic Politics Then and Now

So what is new? Politics, per se, has always been symbolically mediated. Only rarely have we ever experienced politics directly. Even if a politician were to kiss our baby, eat our ethnic food, or wear our funny hat, that would be symbolic. Certainly, post-Civil War politics, when the "bloody flag of rebellion" was for decades waved, were symbolic. And very little in the name of concrete governance (problem solving) came from these symbols (Sundquist, 1973). Reification (taking symbols or names as if they were real objects from nature) has been part of the human condition since the dawn of civilization. But conditions changed. Modernity, however reified are the explanatory systems used to justify it, had more stable metanarratives, which were at least vulnerable to evidence of internal contradiction; there were truth functions available for use by opponents as well as proponents of the status quo.

To bring out the difference, we contrast the view of Frankfurt School philosopher Herbert Marcuse (especially *One Dimensional Man,* 1964) with a postmodern analog. Pretend, counterfactually, that there is a central intelligence steering mechanism for those classes of people (the establishment in Marcuse's terms) advantaged by the status quo. In a modern strategy, the advantaged might have conspired in their clubs, universities, and think tanks to come up with some (hegemonic) system of thought, some logically consistent and relatively stable metanarrative of the world by which the relationships of its parts might, however falsely, be grasped, held, and therefore legitimized. And this metanarrative would be flexible enough at its boundaries to coopt and absorb potential aspects of opposition by reinterpreting them in its own terms. That is essentially Marcuse's theory of one dimensionality, reducing everything that is other to the unidimensional terms of the monolithic metanarrative. Thus wearing old jeans as a gesture of resistance to consumerism is coopted when the market provides new "old" jeans at premium prices. Marcuse's description still resonates; certain rituals of policy pronouncements, like the State of the Union address, still call for metanarrative cooptation. But modern cooptation has been mightily augmented by postmodern strategies.

In the postmodern era, that same counterfactual central intelligence steering committee (the establishment) would have a different strategy, although the goal of gaining acquiescence of others to the favorable status quo would be the same. The establishment would not rely on the old stable metanarrative (of which orthodoxy was a part) because even by the skewed standards set by such a metanarrative, the status quo is amenable to devastating critique. Instead of rescuing the metanarrative, the postmodern condition makes it easier to just continuously divert attention from narratives altogether. Explain not the poverty level, blighted cities, environmental crises, and rates of unemployment or incarceration. Float instead an inexhaustible sequence of unrelated images which pander to more primal fears. Develop instead an endless series of diversionary "plastic disposable reifications" (see Fox & Miller, 1993) to serve as short-lived, prepackaged conceptual gimmicks that evaporate when opened. Instead of promulgating ideological pamphlets, traffic in images which, like Pepsi or Bud Lite advertising campaigns, can be endlessly reproduced when their freshness or media shelf life has expired. We suggest that this was the genius of the Reagan-Bush-Atwater public relations presidencies.[12]

2. The Struggle for Meaning Capture

We neither claim nor think in terms of a conspiracy theory where all actors know what they are doing and where they fit into some master plan. Yet we do want to suggest that something like what is described in the previous subsection is happening. In the struggle for power over the imagination, now made more permeable by the postmodern condition, the individual citizen, a victim of monologue, receives information but cannot shape it. If there is any validity at all to the thinning-of-reality thesis, then voting majorities, especially the swing votes of the least attentive, will have no independent basis from which to judge the veracity of competing political entrepreneurs and their Bud Lite electoral campaigns. No thoughtful policy input can, for the clutter, squeeze its way into the loop. There can be no will formation from the people. The media, which reduce all issues to trivia, regardless of their magnitude, will continue to titillate, distract, and create that self-referential hyperreality which floats ever farther away from governance that might ameliorate actual problems of the lifeworld. Moreover, insofar as neotribalism is true, single-issue voting on symbolic matters will continue to create distracting static and white noise, drowning out any clear signal that may be helpful in shaping policy.

But a number of players do have resources. Bureaucratic elites, journalists, ad creators, political consultants, and intellectuals employed in think tanks or academic institutions have voice. Because the services of individuals practicing these crafts are compensated, it is not unreasonable to assume that those with the power to pay will have asymmetrical capacity in the struggle for meaning capture.[13] Brought into doubt by postmodern monologic communication is the very possibility of the sequence: rational discourse, leading to popular will formation, leading to governance aimed at ameliorating societal problems.

We have linked orthodoxy to both modern and postmodern symbol manipulation, calling into question its democratic claims. Postmodern conditions also vex constitutionalist and communitarian alternatives.

B. UNDOING THE CANONS

As a constitutionally grounded agency, the Public Administration of the Blacksburg tendency is the sort of universalizing claim or grand narrative that postmodernists have been eager to dismiss. Foundationalist claims are but strategically crafted metanarratives.

1. Foundationalism of Constitutionalism

At an intellectual level, anything that attempts to pass itself off, in postmodern conditions, as canonical (like the founding of a constitution or some distant social contract) will be debunked, deconstructed, and dismissed. The radical nominalism of postmodernism is singularly hostile to claims of universality. Such reifications as sovereignty are readily dismissed as hypostatized narrative, claims that cannot be redeemed except by self-reference to one's own particular canon. If constitutionalists assert one version of the founding, the Iroquois can provide a different narrative of how the Constitution came to be. (That is to say, what white Americans take to be the founding was nothing but a plagiarized version of the Iroquois governance structure.) As "reality" continues to mutate rapidly, institutions from a different time, articulated for a different set of purposes, will be dead weight. And the apathetic, instant-karma postmodern citizen is not the only postmodern player unwilling to haul the load on behalf of Western traditions. Insofar as such arrangements are seen to privilege elite groups, the old tradition-bound institutions will lose, not gain, legitimacy. Institutional endurance may well depend not so much on legitimacy as on the deadlock of a political process unable to develop enough power to jettison the old institutions—not what the constitutionalists had in mind.

The critiques of canon that may be applied to constitutionalism also apply to orthodoxy, only moreso because orthodoxy has actually done its service as a dominant metanarrative. Another metanarrative that has performed service is sovereignty, which, through the lens of postmodernism, comes across as another reified artifact, an attempt to create the illusion of certainty.

2. Community as Sovereign

To the extent that "community" replaces "elected officials" in the communitarian/civism model, the loop model remains essentially intact, and the bureaucracy can obey a new sovereign, just as Woodrow Wilson imagined an administrative science would do, neutrally serving Republicans, monarchs, or whatever master. Community, as reified integer, fits just as nicely as any of those. All these legitimizing gambits sanctify their own sovereignty and impute to it a higher reality, the effect/intent of which is to institutionally outmaneuver competing claimants.

The strategy of communitarian/civism advocates is not necessarily to reify an artifact as sovereign, however. Our reading is that community is more often theorized as a cultural development toward egalitarian participation and interaction. But community-as-cultural-development presents a different sort of difficulty if the development of community tends toward incommensurability.

C. TALKING PAST ONE ANOTHER IN SERIALIZED HYPERREALITY

Communitarians want all citizens to be involved because the involvement itself is essential to the full development of their potential as humans. Here community exists as a problematic, not as a done deal (or reified artifact). It needs to be nourished, tended to, and developed. Hopefully, public administrators can facilitate this communitarian involvement, thus fulfilling their own potential. Further, the administrator-as-citizen inoculates the polity against domination by the technocracy. But on the whole, postmodernity is unlikely to promote hope for a mass return of the citizenry to the tasks of governance. It is more likely that increasing percentages of the population will be distracted by the hyperreal spectacle.

A second postmodern problem—more subtle than hyperreal distraction— also threatens the communitarian ideal. Communitarianism may or may not succeed in getting people to the forum—and even if they do, what will they talk about? Communitarianism assumes universality, that everyone will be able to communicate from their different yet similar-enough vantage points. But the existence of similar-enough vantage points is called into question in postmodern conditions. All universals are greeted agnostically. The public conversation is not necessarily, therefore, a war of all against all; it will just not be about anything in particular. In his book on postmodernism and democracy, Botwinick (1993) noted Oakeshott's (1991, pp. 489-490) commentary about this sort of conversation: There is no inquiry, no debate, no agreed-upon grounds for asserting truth claims, no propositions to be tested, no persuasion, no refutation, and no requirement that words connote the same phenomena for everyone. Difference is likely, but disagreement is not relevant. At the lively moments in these conversations, gladiators from factions and various NIMBYs will sally forth with rigidly fixed points of view and rote scripts to deadlock public hearings and prevent authentically discursive consideration of what to do next. Hence postmodern neotribes, unable to communicate effectively one subculture with another, are unable to rescue mass society, or to raise the viscosity of the thin, postmodern hyperreality, or to provide the universal grounding that would transcend neotribalism.

Better to have participation than not, we continue to agree. But in postmodern conditions the responsible communitarian citizenry seems evermore absent and lacking, perhaps altogether inaccessible, and this is the third postmodern problem. When community is reduced to a series of otherwise atomized individuals brought together usually by the coincidence of their consumptive activity, the community does not develop political skills. New England town meetings may evoke nostalgic fantasies of true democracy, but these meetinggoers are not participants. Most of them sit quietly amid a roomful of quasi-strangers and listen to whoever possesses the microphone. The town hall meeting turns out to be another serialized community.

Beyond the serialized community, there are neotribes whose robust discourses tend toward incommensurability with the discourses of other neotribes. If they can be sat down in one place, they still cannot resolve public policy problems. Communitarians can create a new Department of Citizen Participation whose mission it is to promote community involvement, but it matters not what gets discussed. Alas, communitarians are like gamblers: What matters is not the gain nor the loss of money; the thrill is in the wagering.

Are postmodern conditions insurmountable? We do not want to be associated with some deterministic position which claims that we have crossed over some bridge into a *film noir* fantasy world, with no possibility of return. The film *Brazil* is not inexorably our future. We would, however, opine that to whatever extent postmodern consciousness, hyperreality, thin national culture, and neotribalism have validity, orthodoxy and the representative democratic accountability feedback loop are more unsatisfying still, if that is possible, than when we left them at the end of Chapter 2. The alternative of constitutionalism/neoinstitutionalism would be especially unconvincing in an era hostile to canon. Likewise, the idealism of communitarianism, although attractive, seems misplaced given citizen indifference and the questionable status of community. Postmodernity may also defeat discourse and render quixotic our own efforts at a discourse theory of governance. But we have crafted an immune system to some of the viruses infecting other nascent paradigmatic alternatives to orthodoxy. It is time to lay the groundwork for this alternative model.

Notes

1. Anthony Giddens (1990), among others (see, e.g., Jencks, 1991; Suleiman, 1991) makes a strong case that instead of postmodernity, we should regard our current era as radical modernity; modernity extended and attached to a juggernaut careening only potentially out of control. Giddens, a sociologist influential in organization theory, and therefore to be reckoned with in the literature niche we hope to occupy, analyzes contemporary trends through the lens of the "structuration" of relatively viscous institutional structures. We would agree with him, were we not otherwise distracted by the increasingly predominant hyperreality of signs and consciousness influenced by TV, phenomena left largely unexamined or (in our view) underemphasized in his works. Beyond being distracted, our analysis is influenced by the postmodern politics of signs. However, as we define it, the postmodern condition is *mediated* (that is, contained by the concrete universal of the body-subject as described in Chapter 4); hence the difference between postmodern and radical modern may end up being a largely (merely) semantic dispute.

2. Moreover, the oppositional technique is a modernist analytical ploy. Because we do not claim to be postmodernists, we resort to such methods with impunity. More scandalous is the fact that we borrow the postmodernist voice in much of this chapter, only to make use of their insights, which are formidable and need to be reckoned with.

3. Although united by milieu, kinship, and the shared experiences of the group, we will later want to hold out the possibility of some individuation, at least enough so that sufficiently stable standpoints allow for agonistic tension in turn required for discourse.

4. The standpoint assumed by this argument may disturb those who accept their own truths as true in some universal sense. In order to parsimoniously describe postmodernism we must, to a certain extent, assume in advance its triumph over all modern metanarratives; to utter postmodernism is to presuppose the victory of Nietzsche (see, e.g., MacIntyre, 1981, pp. 109-120). We cannot both display the distinction modern/postmodern and at the same time fight battles *within* modernism that we, along with a host of others, have fought elsewhere (see Fox, 1980, 1989).

5. Accessible accounts include Bernstein (1983, 1992). Catholic renditions of the critique of reason, even if to ultimately valorize Aristoteleanism and Thomism, are excellent on the point; see, e.g., MacIntyre (1981) or Jonsen and Toulmin (1988). In the English-speaking world of philosophy, perhaps the most influential of the antifoundationalists have been Ludwig Wittgenstein (1953) and Richard Rorty (1979).

6. It should also be said that the influence of the electronic media on consciousness has been both undertheorized and overtheorized. We don't think that media influences have been paradigmatically understood in their own right. Analysis of broadcast media is normally tacked on to analyses of other linguistic, political, or commercial phenomena to help make or validate points originally arising from some other theoretical problematic—indeed, that is what we are doing. TV, though, is in a category by itself, both vast by itself and exponentially more vast yet when thought of as the media that gathers up all media. Consider only that analysis of the novel occupies thousands of scholars, whereas a TV message is multimedia, voice, printed word, music, two-dimensional art, film, and so on. It is, of course, beyond our project, as well as our ability, to make up for these shortcomings in the scholarship on TV. Important aspects of our analysis rely on Poster (1990). Also important are Kellner (1989, 1990), Baudrillard (1981, 1983), Jamieson (1992), and Jameson (1991).

7. C-SPAN would be at least as monologic as an American government lecture to a class of 1,300; neither talk shows nor "interactive" TV represents an exception to the general monologue.

8. We are alluding to the possibility, not yet empirically established, that TV violence or pornography leads to the increase in real violence, sexual assault, and sexual harassment. It is hypothetically plausible that constant bombardment by grisly images might inure the body-subject to similar phenomenological experiences. It is equally plausible to hypothesize that humans differentiate (and better over time) between TV image and lifeworld phenomena (see Chapter 4 for explication of body-subject).

9. But not in time to affect an infusion of funds to the Department of Defense's anti-ballistic missile research program.

10. Is it perhaps not also true that the current popularity of positive theory, rational/public choice theory, and mathematical modeling is a reaction to the thinning of common "reality"? They, too, are self-referential and removed from the political and policy "realities" of everyday governance. They are codes in Baudrillard's sense: "contemporary theories refer textually primarily to other theories rather than to a 'real' outside" (Kellner, 1989, p. 64).

11. When the Pharmaceutical Manufacturers Association decided to launch a campaign against health care reform, they anted up $850,000 for a six-month advertising campaign and hired Jody Powell, once President Jimmy Carter's press secretary, to strategize a "grass-roots" uprising against price controls on drugs (Levine & Silverstein, 1993).

12. The failure of the Bush reelection campaign may be analyzed in many ways. Many will say, as did the sign at Clinton's Little Rock campaign headquarters, that it was "the economy, stupid." But that sign may be interpreted not as a direct reflection of the reality of economic troubles, but as a more freshly minted epiphenomenon—a plastic disposable reification—than those used by Bush's advertisers. Coke wins over Pepsi this time because the Pepsi ad agency relied on ads whose "shelf-life" had expired. Or consider the double life of the Willie Horton TV ad that devastated Michael Dukakis. It was a simulacrum of his crime policy. Then it became a simulacrum of Republican (Pepsi) negative TV political advertising. The name Willie Horton, as a second-order simulacrum, was actually mentioned twice as often in the 1992 campaign as it was in the one of 1988.

13. Paid-for propaganda finds ample airplay for its unopposed expression. We do not have space to present the sociology of knowledge that would pin down with requisite subtlety the construction of a right-wing literati with credentials sufficient to command national attention through which meaning is captured (but see Edsall & Edsall, 1991; Steinfels, 1979). But however one wishes to measure its magnitude against other expenditures by the rich or against offsetting institutions or sociologies of knowledge which might counterbalance them, movement conservatives associated with the Heritage Foundation, the Olin Foundation, the Joseph Coors Foun-

dation, the Meese Justice Department, and the Rockefellers have themselves been handsomely underwritten and funded, and their books promoted. Right-wing ideological warriors would have been otherwise reduced to the genteel poverty and academic Siberianization that is common to independent warriors less likely to attract such sponsors. It is worth noting also that right-wing commentator Rush Limbaugh does not suffer for lack of corporate sponsors; Jim Hightower, who also has a radio program but is often critical of corporate practices, has not to date been nationally syndicated for want of corporate sponsors.

PART TWO

Discourse Theory

So far, this book has been largely critical. We adduced the arguments against orthodoxy. We were not entirely pleased with the constitutionalist/neoinstitutionalist alternative. We thought civism to be an unlikely solution despite the ideal strengths of its communitarian underpinnings. Our excursion into postmodernity and postmodernism raised even more doubts about public administration/policy, but especially about the environment in which it must function, and frankly, it makes the construction of yet another alternative a daunting task. Although we believe our critiques to be telling, able to stand on their own, we take up now the more challenging task of developing a normative[1] theory of public administration/policy.

From our perspective a normative theory with sufficient fecundity to be worth doing should have the following assets. First, it should have an epistemological/ontological stance sensitive to what we accept as the devastating critique made by postmodern thinkers against foundationalism, universalism, metanarratives, and reified canons. Second, it must nevertheless be constructive and positive; we aspire to midwifery, not funeral directing. Third, although reaching beyond the given, a normative theory should still be based on possibilities that are already extant. That is, from given practices, we want to tease out positive or emancipatory potential, and by valorizing them within a normative theory, affirm them—we seek a balance between tough-minded realism about the present and a nonutopian vision of incrementally improving it.

We think that the way to do this is to take up a strain of thought begun, but then abandoned, by Jürgen Habermas (1992, p. 442). Habermas is clearly one of the most profound, influential, and prolific thinkers of our time. He is also singular in including public administration problematics, in more than just passing, in his work. An early book of his, *The Structural Transformation of the Public Sphere,* only recently translated into English (Habermas, 1989), presents evidence of relatively authentic discourse by public-spirited bourgeois European males in the 18th and 19th centuries. It was undermined by the forces of mass culture, the extremes of which we have sketched as postmodernity in Chapter 3. Habermas suggested that a public sphere, constituted by a deliberatively informed public opinion, might be recaptured by the literate, the interested, the informed, and the engaged, augmented mightily by the mass of those now peopling public sector organizations. But, he writes,

> To be able to satisfy these functions in the sense of democratic opinion and consensus formation their [public sector organizations'] inner structure must first be organized in accord with the principle of publicity [i.e., deliberatively determined public interest] and must institutionally permit an intra-party or inter-association democracy—to allow for unhampered communication and public rational-critical debate. (Habermas, 1989, p. 209; cited by Calhoun, 1992, p. 28)

We suggest that public policy and administration exhibit nascent tendencies which may, upon fruition, meet these criteria. Because they lay hidden under the reified perceptual overlay of orthodox presuppositions, we need to peel away those presuppositions to see them. Brought to light, these nascent discursive practices can be affirmed and embraced when understood as democratic transformative nodes in energy fields.

Now Habermas never himself pursued this possibility and instead articulated a neo-Kantian ideal of authentic communication, that is, discourse driven by the internal logic of communication and language to pursue justice and equality. Ingenious by modernist/enlightenment standards, such an ideal has rightly been criticized as one of those self-validating foundational universals, a basis for a metanarrative, that are anathema to the postmoderns. Much of his effort these last few years has been spent defending what he admits is an enlightenment/modernist vision against the postmoderns. We, on the other hand, want to take up the original argument and avoid the foundation-alist quagmire into which Habermas fell after he gave up that practical position for a more purely deontological one. We think the precondi-tion for such discourse that he mentioned—interassociation democ-racy—is at least nascently, potentially, germinating today in extrabu-reaucratic policy networks and other formations.[2]

Our aim, then, is to explore the possibility of authentic discourse that includes our (public administration) ranks *but without* falling into foundationalist traps. We want practical aspects of the Habermasian ideal, but we do not think we have to affirm, as he has done, discred-ited modernist strategies to do it. The business at hand, then, is first to sketch a nonfoundationalist framework from which discourse can be affirmed. That is the job of Chapter 4. We will then be ready, in Chapter 5, to outline (again leaning on Habermas) the ideal require-ments for such discourse. Finally, in Chapter 6, we will use our standards to assay a series of current practices to applaud those aspects that lead to discourse and warn against ways that they violate the spirit of authentic discourse.

Notes

1. But a theory not normative in either a deontological or teleological sense. Regard this as a kind of social constructivist "small n" normative guide to viewing lifeworld phenomena; we mean to advance a way of interpreting phenomena in ways that may help valorize aspects of them, thereby encouraging the movement of recursive practices in those directions.

2. Habermas, though, at this point, held out a hope, which we take up as a pregnant suggestion insufficiently explored by him. It is the one suggested by the 1960s slogan "the long march through the institutions" (Calhoun, 1992, pp. 27-29). After staffing the barricades, shouting at LBJ, and getting jailed in Birmingham and attacked by police in Chicago in 1968, it occurred to public-spirited dissidents that a more careerist alternative, working within the system and reforming it from within, was a perhaps more sensible path. The styles and views of such people would have had influence, sending out vectors of momentum in the energy field.

4 Theoretical Underpinnings of Discourse Theory

*Phenomenology, Constructivism,
Structuration Theory, and Energy Fields*

I. Theoretical Base

This chapter has three moments. First, we appropriate what we take to be cutting-edge philosophy and social theory to develop an arsenal of vocabulary and concepts to allow the valorization of discourse theory. We seek to disseminate new eyeglasses, the lenses of which allow for an altered view of the public administration field. This is the constructivist moment and includes excursions into phenomenology, constructivism, and structuration theory. In the second moment, we take up these newly forged tools for the purpose of deconstructing the traditional (reified) concepts that now (mis)channel our attention to bureaucratic structures. Finally, third, we suggest an alternative conceptual scheme, the public energy field, which transcends and subtends existing institutions, organizations, and bureaucracy.

A. WHY WE NEED INNOVATIVE "CONSTRUCTIVIST" SOCIAL THEORY

As we begin to try to theorize ourselves out of the cul-de-sac of postmodernism, we can appreciate the pragmatic virtues of denial—it is comforting to think that nothing fundamental has changed. The orthodox paradigm and its alternatives have been rendered obsolete by forces that can as easily defeat anything we might offer up. Having ourselves helped mine the field, we must now try to tiptoe through it without making "pink mist" of the positive contribution we want to make. If "reality" is increasingly ephemeral, how can we capture enough of it to tease out credible suggestions about what to do next? By what means can the serial incommensurabilites of neotribal surety be made amenable to democratic deliberations? More specifically, why do we think a discourse theory is at least a conceptually valid response to the situation in which we find ourselves?

The simple answer to the last question is that discourse theory allows affirmation of, and may, when properly theorized, induce improvements in, tendencies already extant in public administration. We want ultimately to valorize proactive participation of public administrators intermingled with others of public-minded communities in policy networks, interagency consortia, adhocracies, and task forces. These we take to be the appropriate loci for a potential public sphere. Such extralegislative policy forums, as the literature on "iron triangles" exemplifies, are, however, rendered through the lenses of orthodoxy as thefts of sovereignty—more, the ascendance of technocracy. Although we have laid some licks on orthodoxy and its alternatives, we require a newly engineered epistemology/ontology to affirm a discourse alternative. It is to this matter that we first turn. To associate ourselves with a broader tendency under which students of public administration can classify us, we will call it constructivism.[1]

Constructivism has this simple message: Organizational reality, what public administrators experience as the flux and flow of daily life, is socially constructed. Because organizational reality is not imposed by some impersonal or material force outside of human groups, it is amenable to adjustment by human groups. The reality of our daily lives is historically contingent. Humans are not just wafted about by impersonal forces beyond their control. Institutions R us. If all of us were to perish at once, or experience universal lobotomy, institutions would vanish along with our memory traces. That this simple message should seem counterintuitive to so many is explicable by the commonsense Western assumption about individual selves (what we will refer to as atomistic individuals): There is me inside, then there is everything else outside. Me is subjective, outside is objective. I react and adjust to it. Philosophy, understood as a kind of concept therapy (Wittgenstein, 1953; see also Fox, 1992, p. 3), can help overcome this naive commonsensical view.

But therapy is expensive; in this case the currency is reader effort. We need an altered and extended vocabulary in order to transcend what many would agree to be an unsatisfactory predicament for public administration/policy. It's not as if we have to invent these terms (although there will be a bit of that); rather we need to familiarize or remind readers in our literature of words and concepts that are being developed in other literatures. We want ultimately to be able to say such things as: The word *bureaucracy* only partially connotes what we do, only partially describes the way we do it, and fits scarcely at all with our aspirations. *Discourse,* we will want to say, fits our aspirations. To say such things credibly, we need to break through the conceptualizations surrounding *bureaucracy* and *institution,* to see what they are made of. We will make this as painless as possible, but it will require some effort for members of the public administration community to appropriate the conceptual tools, developed in other communities, required to theorize our way out of that postmodern predicament which now counts as the external environment of public administration/policy. We begin by articulating a philosophical base in phenomenology leading up to constructivism and structuration theory.

B. PHENOMENOLOGICAL UNDERPINNINGS OF CONSTRUCTIVISM

In this discourse theory of public administration, we are urging movement away from the idea that there is a reality "out there" that a value-free researcher can account for by formulating law-like generalizations whose veracity is observable, testable, and cumulative. We reject the notion that the "What is?" question can be addressed credibly only by objective observers, as the emphasis on neutral science would prescribe. Merely asking one question rather than some other question betrays some measure of subjectivity. If disinterestedness were required, there would be no inquiry. We acknowledge that the positivist project and its methodology have some validity; but exclusive reliance on it occludes many phenomena available to human perception (see Fox, 1990). In Chapter 3, when we distinguished between denotative (the definitional signifier) and connotative meanings (the contextual meaning that depends on experiences or interrelated conditions), we were also beginning to draw distinctions between (a) the view that statements or propositions are confirmable by observation and (b) the view that any statements or propositions contain presuppositions and are themselves conditioned by the context.

1. The Body Subject: Undoing Dichotomous Thought

In order to reconceptualize the self and its relationship to the world one must, in a sense, go back and redo the Cartesian cogito (I think, therefore I am) which is the intellectual antecedent of our current difficulties (Merleau-Ponty, 1962, p. ix). We must attempt to get beyond, behind, and below the reified abstractions of thought to our shared and indubitable experience of life.

> The first philosophical act would appear to be a return to the world of actual experience, which is prior to the objective world, because it is in it that we shall be able to grasp the theoretical basis no less than the limits of that objective world, restore to things their concrete physiognomy, to organisms their individual ways of dealing with the world, and to subjectivity its inherence in history. (Merleau-Ponty, 1962, p. 57)

In other words, when the requirements of reified categories of thought are set aside, what remains as precategorical and prephilosophical is but a corporeal self and its field of activity. According to Merleau-Ponty, what will be discovered in the "world of actual experience" is the body-subject and its world. What distinguishes the embodied self from pure mind is this physical locus: There is this body for which meanings develop. Preconscious bodily meaning is not some mystical, darkly Freudian, or occult meaning, but the simple not-having-to-think-about-it-meaning of normal everyday experience. The following example is illustrative.

We are walking together and we are engaged in a heated discussion about political matters. As we walk, so engaged, we avoid trees, watch for cars, step over curbs, walk up steps, enter a room, spot an unoccupied table, walk to it, pull out a couple of chairs and take seats. Only comedian Chevy Chase's slapstick characters cannot accomplish the task of walking and chewing gum at the same time. For the most part, we operate at a preconscious, prepersonal, and precategorical level; we do not have to affirm consciously the existence of the chair we pull out to sit on. This is what Merleau-Ponty means by the preconscious bodily orientation. It is a basic dimension ignored by orthodox psychology and philosophy.

It must be made clear that the elucidation of the tacit dimension does not deny the conscious level. Indeed, a hard and fast distinction between these would be erroneous, for "consciousness is a network of significative intentions which are sometimes clear to themselves and sometimes, on the contrary, lived rather then known" (Merleau-Ponty, 1963, p. 173).

2. Intentionality in Situations: The Question of What to Do Next?

Intentionality is often said to be the chief theme of phenomenology. As it is usually conceived, intentionality is the name for Husserl's (1962) insight that consciousness cannot be considered apart from its contents. Consciousness is consciousness of . . . of something. Consciousness is not an empty container; it is predicated. Consciousness has always some thing, an immanent object, to which it points.[2] Intentionality, as it is most generally meant, is the synthetic act of consciousness by which the phenomenon is made to be.

But Husserl's view teeters on the brink of idealism.[3] Idealism has always been able to make the powers of consciousness intelligible—that is its virtue—but only by losing contact with the density and fecundity of worldly being. Husserl gives us a consciousness filled to the brim with *its* objects, but their origin remains obscure. But, according to Samuel Mallin (1979),

> Merleau-Ponty's philosophy may be characterized as a philosophy of situation. Situation is the most comprehensive term Merleau-Ponty uses to express the ultimate unity of man with his surroundings, and thus it is fundamental to the discussion of aspects of his epistemology and metaphysics. The sense of situation in which we are interested is roughly synonymous with "involvement in circumstances" or "active concern with sets of natural, cultural, or human problems." (p. 1)

Merleau-Ponty wants to further remedy the idealist disconnection with the situation by giving to the "consciousness of action" a home in the broader subjectivity which is the body.

A direct result of adding the body to epistemological inquiry is a shift in the meaning of *subject* and *subjectivity*. The body and the subject are joined as *body-subject,* indicating a distance between traditional conceptualizations of subjectivity and that of Merleau-Ponty. The Cartesian view has consciousness at the center of subjectivity, which, as one would expect, both conforms to and reinforces the traditional dichotomization of mind and matter. Merleau-Ponty spreads subjectivity, previously concentrated as mind, throughout body, giving corporeality to subjectivity. Hence it must be the body itself as a whole with consciousness, reflexes, and sedimented habitual comportments, with all of its senses and powers pulling together, which is the appropriate unit to consider. Our bodies participate in linking us to the environment, enabling us to have knowledge of the world. Our bodies are not locked into a narrow set of interactions as are, say, a golden retriever's, and even the golden retriever has a broader range of possibilities than does a frog. In all cases, however—frog, dog, and human—the body helps synthesize meaning (of insects, a pat on the head, or tone of voice). Before intellectual engagement there exists a certain primordial contact with the world that joins in the shaping of our perceptions, helping to organize the perceptual field and giving definition to the situation in which we find ourselves. The sensory input of each situation does not impinge on a blank slate (as it would in Cartesian and Lockean object-subject dualism); rather there are *givens* that we bring to each situation, such as the givens that predispose us to perceive a cube when we can see only three of its sides (Whiteside, 1988).

Our first experience with cubes contributed to our lived experience, helping to frame our next encounter with a cube. Each situation contributes something to the sedimented meanings that structure the next moment. Although the mental structures embedded in this sedimented lifeworld place limits on the mind's ability to alter meaning, they also enable the body-subject to engage in dialogue with each fresh situation. Thus the object-subject dualism of the Cartesian system and the dichotomous thinking it has engendered ever since, was a serious error, with lasting consequences. In place of an objective-subjective dichotomized reality, there is a body-subject of sedimented experience that confronts new situations.

Merleau-Ponty described how mental structures condition perception in ways not appreciated through either empiricism or idealism (Whiteside, 1988). He questioned how a cube could exist, from an empiricist standpoint, because one can see only three sides. The synthesis that is required to complete the cube is not available in a strict empirical regimen. From an idealist standpoint, what the observer sees is mere appearance, a function of the mind, and the cube need not actually exist as such. A third way is available. From a phenomenological standpoint, the complete cube is clarified by differences in light on the three sides and by the mind's ability to see with perspective, leading to an immediate reference with minimal intellectual effort. Moreover, after we have investigated our first cube, child's play with blocks, all subsequent cubes are easy to synthesize without having to pick them up, or walk around to the other side. Just as each new cube is now prefigured in our minds, our lifeworld reaching out before us is also suggestively prefigured by sedimented givens or mental structures. We begin the present with things already partially given.

This move to give corporeal in-the-world grounding to subjectivity gives substance to the notion of intentionality. Intentionalities are the active voluntarist sparks emanating from body-subjects. Intentionalities shape perception itself. From the infinite possibilities of figure and ground configurations possible at the intersection of subject and world at any moment, a particular one is chosen. This is not determined from the outside but codetermined by a field of possibilities and individual appropriation of a given concatenation of them. All of the corporeal subject's senses, beginning with preconscious awareness, combining along an intentional beam, add up not to the mere "I observe" of traditional views; they add up to an "I am able" (Merleau-Ponty, 1962, p. 137). We do not only observe the properties of an external world, but we inhabit the world as a field of potentialities for our actions. This is the meaning of motility. Thus what is accomplished by Merleau-Ponty's innovation is the breakdown of the distinction between perception and action.

The body-subject does not perceive or observe in some instances and then act in other, entirely distinct, instances. Preconscious intentionality describes a more fundamental realm in which perception is, in the very first instance, for action. Dialectically, action is also for perception. Action is not separate from sense making; indeed, sense making is for action. Action is a physical expression of intentionality, conditioned by the sense one makes of the situation. This is relevant for our project because as a sense-making process, discourse pins down the possibilities for meanings and transforms phenomena into utterances, words and signs, intentions, social currency . . . and *action*.

Because we are born and raised in human culture, because we assimilate the language of our human environment, a precondition for competent acting in the world, we do not come to each new present moment empty-handed. Whereas in the past we have been accustomed to separating object from subject, mind from nature, and ideas from material reality, phenomenology asks us to take a different tack. "We must recognize a sort of sedimentation of our life: an attitude toward the world, when it has received frequent confirmation acquires a favoured status for us" (Merleau-Ponty, 1962, p. 441). Any engagement begins in preconstituted circumstances—a particular setting of sound, light, and ambience encumbered by the concerns, emotions, and interests of those in attendance, and in the context of mental structures, meanings, predispositions, and expectations that people bring to the situation. The investigator, too, initiates movement, experiences feelings, and takes action. Not even a logical positivist investigator can stand apart from these conditions nor ignore their historicity. Our perceptive capacity is not so passive as to merely observe; we also choose and select among sensory data, we form structures in our minds, and we evaluate that with which our intentionality has merged. We focus awareness and ascribe meanings to events that they otherwise would not possess. We develop new structures of thought, which themselves become sedimented. With our capacity to synthesize sedimented meanings, it takes no intellectual effort to recognize a pile of stones as a "wall," to hear a succession of sounds as "music," to recognize a gesture of the hand as an attempt at communication. . . . Human life takes place, for the most part, in a world of human construction. (Whiteside, 1988, pp. 74-75)

We constantly create culture by creating a nonnatural world that nonetheless feels natural (Whiteside, 1988). This world we live in is one of our own making. Although we are not culturally determined, we are culturally conditioned. As Merleau-Ponty (1962) put it, "I am situated in a social environment, and my freedom, though it may have the power to commit me elsewhere, has not the power to transform me instantaneously into what I decide to be" (p. 447).

3. Summing Up Phenomenological Insights

Phenomenology provides us with four conceptual tools necessary for a discourse theory. They are *very* important.

1. The *body-subject* is simultaneously both physical and mental. Our bodies literally in*corp*orate objectivity and subjectivity. And, because all consciousness occurs in bodies, with significant overlapping capacities with all other similar bodies, we will ultimately be able to foil incorrigible incommensurability. Discourse is possible, neotribalism need not, in principle, prevail because of this concrete universal.

2. *Intentionality* sparks out from body-subjects-in-the-world, not just for idle contemplation or interested observation, but for the motility, for the action, of those body-subjects. This too, gives to all bodies an irreducible commonality. Regarding the other walking toward me, I recognize the subtle clues that she intends to pass me on the left. I recognize the intentionality of that perceiving body-subject, that alter-ego with comportments similar to my own.

3. Intentionality sparks out from body-subjects bearing the marks of their time, class, gender, and place. Lived-in body-subjects acquire *sedimented habitual comportments,* favored styles of living-in-the-world, which taken in aggregate make up infinitely varied but uniquely authentic selves.

4. Body subjects are always *situated*. The Cartesian imagination may wander where it will, but in cases of competent human actors, consciousness always comes home to the situated body-subject-in-the-world.

C. CONSTRUCTIVISM

Ontology is about being or existence. The flip side of an ontology is epistemology, which is about what and how humans might know or acquire knowledge of being or existence. Traditionally—that is, in the history of philosophy—the two are separated, even as tradition affirms that they imply each other. For the social world of everyday life (we leave aside, or as philosophers say, "bracket," physical reality which is beyond our problematic), a constructivist view combines, telescopes, ontology and epistemology. This move is made possible by the insight that humans who seek to know social reality are themselves the carriers of it. Observers of social reality cannot be external to it, nor can their observations be incorrigibly isolated from that being observed. Conceptions of this reality, then, are, in a sense negotiated. This is called the social construction of reality by Berger and Luckmann (1966), and their hugely influential book by that title is what gives constructivism its name.

Accordingly, a constructivist epistemology/ontology is radically nominalist. The names we (interactive human groups) give things are ultimately arbitrary. They could be any combination of grunts, tongue clicks, and gestures. Names, symbols, are not so much denotative of some*thing* as they are socially agreed-upon gestures, various shorthand significations, for commonly accepted aspects of the lifeworld of that group for which significance has been mutually developed.

Lifeworld, in turn (would that we could say everything at once), is a term essential to constructivism. Originated by Husserl (*lebenswelt*) in the early 20th century, lifeworld is a construct developed not so much to transcend as to get to the experiential base of reified categorical thought (see Kockelmans, 1967). The human ability and tendency to reify ("thingify," or make real) can, over time, create thought patterns so grandiose that they obscure the daily practices of life from which these categories were primordially derived. The term *bureaucracy*, as we will argue below, is just such a reification and gets in the way of explication of lifeworld practices. Such reifications then tend to ignore, even deny, the most obvious evidence arising from the lifeworld. A lifeworld perspective is one eternally vigilant against such reifications, asking at every turn the relevance of theoretical constructs to the intersecting intentionalities and projects of body-subjects in groups as they are lived from moment to moment and day to day. Consistent attending to lifeworld imperatives, by the way, would be a large measure of prevention against such organizational pathologies as goal displacement.

Intentionalities, again, are the active voluntarist sparks emanating from individuals. Constructivism would have intentionality replace motivation of standard views. Motivation implies the stimulus-response behavioralist psychology, which represents people as rats. Stimulate the rat (shocks = stick, food = carrot), and it will respond. Correspondingly, motivate the human, that is, provide stimulus from the outside to elicit desired responses from the organismic inside otherwise thought to be at rest, and appropriate (to management) organizational performance can be summoned. Outside motivational incentives or rewards, as in Weber's bureaucracy and Downs's and rational choice theories, are thought to remediate pathologies caused by inappropriate incentives and rewards. We note in passing that stimulus-response conceptions of motivation cannot in principle be falsified. If a particular stimulus or combination of stimuli fail to extract desired behaviors, there are an almost infinite number of new combinations to try out. In this way the ghost of Taylorism can reappear 50 years after its burial dressed in the shrouds of expectancy theory.

Intentionality, on the other hand, assumes individuals with projects. To be sure, that individual is not the autonomous, unembodied, acultural individual of the Cartesian cogito (I think, therefore I am), but it is, with all of the variegated sediments which it embodies, gathers up, and projects forward, a subject with autonomous choices. This subject is capable of more than predictable response to the external manipulation of rewards; it is capable indeed of discourse. Intentionality is, then, the more immediate term—what the active subject has as its immediate objective with respect to the situation at hand. Projects organize and direct intentionalities over the long term; a project encompasses the past accumulation of intentionalities in the present, forecast to the future. A project is an intimation of a lifeswork seen at the juncture referred to as now, or the present situation. We intend this sentence to communicate meaning. Doing so is part of the project of doing a book, itself part of the project to advance discourse.

D. CONSTRUCTIVISM AND STRUCTURATION THEORY

The foregoing paragraphs on intentionality, projects, and lifeworld may be regarded as appropriate (but not exclusive) vocabulary to describe the proclivities of human subjects—the voluntarist side of things affirmed by constructivism and such similar intellectual traditions as phenomenology, hermeneutics, interpretivism, ethnomethodology, and others. There is, however, another entire tradition of the social sciences that attempts to grasp systems, the dynamics of whole societies, cultures, and economies. Structuralism, functionalism, Parsonianism, systems theory, social Darwinism, dialectical materialism, Hegelian Marxism, and macroeconomics are some examples. In our own discipline of public administration, the grand narratives of Weber, James Q. Wilson, and Anthony Downs exemplify a systems orientation. One might be inclined, as are some postmodernists, to simply dismiss such grand theories as impossible attempts to conceptualize the whole or totality: How could any puny, mortal, historico-culturally situated and limited human presume to such a thing? To thus dismiss, though, risks justifiable banishment from the field of public administration. One cannot simply ignore agencies, institutions, bureaucracies, and constitutional regimes. One needs to be able to talk about "systematics," but one also needs a way of talking about them that avoids reifying them—making them into immutable things. As sociological theorist Anthony Giddens (1984) remarks:

> The reification of social relations, or the discursive "naturalization" of the historically contingent circumstances and products of human action, is one of the main dimensions of ideology in social life. (p. 26)

Giddens wants to avoid giving to human constructions the immutability that, for instance, the "movement of tectonic plates" represents for Californians residing along the San Andreas fault. We believe that such a way of accounting for systematics without demeaning the subject-active-voluntarist side required for constructivism can be found in the theory of structuration brilliantly developed by Giddens (1984). As he puts it:

> One of my principle ambitions in the formulation of structuration theory is to put an end to each of these empire-building endeavors [e.g., both one-sided voluntarism of hermeneutics, et al., and one-sided reification of systems]. The basic domain of study of the social sciences, according to the theory of structuration, is neither the experience of the individual actor, nor the existence of any form of societal totality, but social practices ordered across space and time. (p. 2)

To avoid overemphasizing either pole of determination, Giddens proposes the term *structuration.*

E. RECURSIVE PRACTICES

Crucial to structuration theory is an understanding of *recursive,* obviously, reoccurrence time and again. Recursive is related to habit, or what Merleau-

Ponty would formulate as embodied cultural sediments. Recursive activities "are not brought into being by social actors but continually recreated by them via the very means whereby they express themselves *as* actors" (Giddens, 1984, p. 2). Humans are born into a world already rich in meanings, which they take up and in doing so re-create or reproduce them, although never exactly identically, for the present and into the future. Now humans exhibit reflexivity (i.e., self-consciousness of actions, intentionalities, and the relationship between these to projects) about their recursive habitual actions, but that reflexivity is not applied in a vacuum (implied again by the cogito: I think, therefore I am) but within the flow of action and interaction within determinable limits. These limits are formed by the expectations of others and cocreated by competent selves grasping, accepting, and performing within the limits of those expectations. Such competent performances reinforce and validate those limits, which become structures of varying strength and duration.

Although recursive practices channel and limit human creativity, it is important to also emphasize that they are the occasions for its exercise. Language, itself a pattern of recursive practices, exemplifies the point. Speaking a language means employing particular words and phrases from a rich stock of potential expressions and deploying them according to a more limited stock of grammatical formulae. There are limits to what a particular stock can provide, but it is difficult to imagine, to think outside of that stock (some philosophies would hold it impossible), that which cannot be expressed. Language limits the speakable, but it is also the means by which we speak. Another way of putting this is to use Merleau-Ponty's distinction based on de Saussure between used language and language in use. Used language is the stock of culturally available linguistic resources. Language in use is the deployment of these resources in communication (see Fox, 1989). Similar patterns can be found in other recursive practices.

It bears repeating here in this context that rules are recursive practices like language. Actors in contemporary agencies, after years of attempts to control their behaviors, will have as a stock more rules than they can possibly apply or attend to. A particular concatenation of rules will be used by groups that have worked out the ones most important to please a particular boss, to accomplish the implementation of a particular interpretation of mission, or just to get through their day.

Recursivity is important because it neither denies nor demeans human agency. It only recognizes that such agency does not spark out in infinite directions at each moment. Indeed, it only rarely wanders from well-worn paths. Nonetheless, as rivers carve out new beds, so may human behavior in the aggregate change course and incrementally rework recursive patterns. A trivial example has to do with professional dress. The computer software industry, located in the so-called Silicon Valley of California, operated in a buyer's market for talent and was led by youthful inventors/entrepreneurs sufficiently confident in their identities to ignore the normal protocols of business dress. Jeans, sweats, and sneakers replaced the traditional business attire of suits, ties, and wingtips. Haircuts optional. Such epicenters of change and role fan out in vectors of momentum (discussed below in energy fields), influencing other evolving patterns of adjusting recursive patterns.

Such changes, in turn, can and usually do occur as the unintended consequences of marginally adjusted recursive practices aggregated as a social pattern. Governance, and the discourse way of actualizing it, may be regarded as conscious mutually reflexive attempts at regulating or directing the marginal adjustments of otherwise randomly developing shifts in recursive practices.

By this (we think accurate) view,

> Social systems, as reproduced social practices, do not *have* "structures" but rather exhibit "structural properties" and that structure exists, as time-space presence, only in its instantiations [manifestations] in such practices and as memory traces orienting the conduct of knowledgeable human agents. (Giddens, 1984, p. 17, italics added).

In other words, systems, institutions, and the like owe their existence not to some objective realm outside the social practices of individuals in groups, but within them. In short, social reality is socially constructed or constantly socially renewed by human behavior patterns regulated by recursive practice. Remembering our radically nominalist stance, we are ready to attach names to recursive patterns of different degrees of duration. Fad and fashion are recursive practices of short and intentionally shifting duration. The joy of variety seems a human trait. Fad and fashion are largely harmless ways to exercise it. At the other extreme, following Giddens (1984, p. 17), "the most deeply embedded structural properties, implicated in the reproduction of societal totalities, [are called] *structural principles.*" Further, "those practices which have the greatest time-space extension within such totalities can be referred to as *institutions.*"

Rooting social structures in recursive practices of varying duration and solidity opens up already fruitful explicatory schemes to further development without some of the distortions that may be associated with them. Regime norms can be subsumed with more bountiful result under structural principles. Institutions and agencies can be subsumed under the expanded understanding of institutionalization articulated by structuration theory. In both cases finding broader sources for these theoretical constructs allows for the appropriate flexibility to reassess (for the purposes of embracing discourse) what are taken to be rigid limitations.

We take Giddens's *structural principles* to be the theoretical equivalent of John Rohr's *regime norms*: those biases toward freedom, equality, and property (Rohr, 1989). We regard it as a superior formulation because it is not limited to formal manifest norms, the regime as it understands itself, written up in official documents and nostalgically traced back to a founding. Structural principles can include such constructs as class society and the way it is reproduced: profit, capital, labor, family structures, educational systems, and the like. An equally important contrast is that regime norms have no mechanism for actualizing themselves into the present beyond study of Supreme Court decisions, hardly a universal practice. The theory of regime norms lacks vessels for their actualization. Structural principles, alternatively, have loci in recursive practices, carried out by socialized individuals. Lest such finding of loci seem overly facile we hasten to admit that from the inside of the isolated individual, structural principles do look fixed, and in a way they are. It is difficult enough for one to overcome one's own habits of thought and action, much less confront the combined sedimented habitual comportments of others in mass. But that does not make them external to human intervention; that does not make of them an ontologically external monolith.

F. INSTITUTIONS ARE HABITS

Understanding institutions is the most important aspect of structuration theory for our purposes. Following Giddens, institutions are recursive practices sustained by resource appropriation and rules. Rules may be of many kinds, certainly not limited to written rules, laws, or standard operating procedures. Rules may be typed according to their profile across a series of bands between the paired polarities of: intensive-shallow, tacit-discursive, informal-formalized, weakly sanctioned-strongly sanctioned (Giddens, 1984, p. 22). Notice the potential for variability and ambiguity here. Although they seem stable when viewed as a whole and seen as a cluster of recursive practices, when viewed at a level of detail, one sees microprocesses and particular rules adjusting to face-to-face encounters, to interpersonal relations within cliques, and to departmental relations. In other words, one sees the evolutionary transformation of recursive practices amid the detail of everyday life. This indeed is precisely the way that specialized jargons develop within groups. Institutions of structuration theory, it follows, are not like institutions of the Weberian idealtype: unalterable slots impervious to the human beings inhabiting them. Such insights are, of course, the stuff of literature on organizational culture (Ingersoll & Adams, 1992; Ott, 1989).

What we want to stress here is the ever-present potential for institutional malleability. If a given reality is socially constructed, that reality can, and inevitably will, be socially reconstructed. The inevitable evolution of recursive practices usually happens as the result of unintended consequence and the permeability of given clusters of recursive practices to changes initiated elsewhere. But these may also be adjusted by discursive will formation, as the Organizational Development (OD) movement has shown in countless empirical instances. OD practices are, of course, themselves based on constructivist insights (Coch & French, 1948).

Hence any given social construction of reality (i.e., that which gathers up and interactively or reciprocally transforms intentions and projects within lifeworld groups) may occur within what are now regarded as institutions. This means that the symbols *institution* and *institutionalize* signify contingent, not permanent for-now-and-all-time, solidification. The degree of institutional fixity will vary greatly, but it can never be absolute. Institutions are habits, not things. Institutions might look the same from decade to decade from the outside, but their practices must surely vary according to the individual intentionalities and the admixtures of same that compose the inside of it. From generation to generation the admixture itself will change radically as social sediments, embodied in individuals and projected outward from them as intentionalities, shift. Certain gestalt formulations within presumed institutionally fixed structures will actually change the institution itself, even as it goes by the same name and presents for public view the same reified face.

The end result is that "human history is created by intentional activities but is not an intended project" (Giddens, 1984, p. 27); or to paraphrase Marx, humanity makes history, but never just as they please. Discourse may be thought of as the attempt to be more proactively interventionist in the at least marginal adjustment of those recursive practices over which influence may be exerted.

We have been developing a constructivist standpoint with a structuration amendment because we need to be able to affirm that reified institutions and

and agencies are transcendable, and also be able to affirm policy networks, interagency consortia, citizen-agency task forces, and the like. This is because over (often very little) time, these latter nascent discursive forms also develop recursive practices of sufficient solidity to qualify as instances of institutionalization. (To anticipate, it is the institutionalization of discursive practices that we seek.) This is to say that two meanings of institution need to be kept in mind. Brass-nameplate institutions contain within themselves many instances of robust institutionalized recursive practices. But relatively stable over time institutionalized recursive practices also exist between brass-nameplate institutions and others of their kind, as well as under, over, and around them. Put another way, stable patterns of recursive practices are too often regarded as formations that are a monopoly of bureaus, agencies, and other formal-legal structures that use the sign *institution* as a synonym for their formal name (as in "this institution").

We also want to blur, and make permeable, what are often taken to be the fixed boundaries between public administration—the bureaucracy—and its clientele (or recently) its customers. One needs to be able to draw a distinction between institutions and agencies, taken on the one hand as boxes on an organization chart written in budget allocations or textbooks, and on the other hand, institutions understood as structurations. Let's try out our new bag of tricks on bureaucracy. After immanent critique of bureaucracy, we will be in position to resituate practices currently thought of as bureaucratic within energy fields.

II. Using Constructivism to Deconstruct the "Conflated Aggregation" Bureaucracy

Again, affirming discourse requires that some old ways of categorizing phenomena be adjusted. *Bureaucracy* is a term that does not capture the totality of public sector activity. This term may be regarded as a reified conflated aggregation, by which we mean a symbol that gathers up diverse and often contradictory lifeworld experiences and peremptorily subsumes them under that symbol. We need to unpack, disaggregate—or in postmodern terminology, *deconstruct*—the conflated aggregation, the mind-numbing category, of bureaucracy. For instance, what does it mean, in the debate over the Clinton Administration's comprehensive health care reform, to say that it will increase bureaucratization? In what way can the conscious discursive attempt to change some institutionalized recursive practices and promote alternative ones be regarded as bureaucratization?

Properly practiced, deconstruction is no mere tribalistic dismissal of alien views. It requires a tracing to the roots of a thing, a genealogy or archeology, so that they can be laid bare. A genealogy of bureaucracy, with Weber as chief herald, reveals rational, control-oriented organizations committed to a mechanistic, cause-and-effect deterministic methodology. Subsequent social science amendments to this model are represented by the probabilistic frame of reference, a strong challenge to determinism despite its close epistemological affinity. Scholars adopted more sophisticated statistical methodologies, enabling them to better account for the complexity and multiplicity of variables. Tendency statements and correlations displaced causality as the aspiration of inquiry. The probabilistic model allowed, too, the realization that the stuff we count and measure is not so concrete as the deterministic model had supposed; rather hypotheses and variables are the constructions of the inquirers or the literature/tradition in which they work. Moreover, the lesson of the so-called Hawthorne effect was that the investigator is part of the problematic and thus interacts with the subject of inquiry. We then go on to argue that the logically next step in epistemological evolution is the constructivist approach that we have already sketched at the level of epistemology/ontology. We will see that when the constructivist approach is applied to it, a bureaucracy is neither a concrete entity nor a self-surviving organism (Pfeffer, 1981). Accordingly, bureaucracy is no longer a term that appropriately subsumes sufficiently fixed practices as to have rational-critical utility. Bureaucracy, in consequence, is more of a rhetorical gambit in the game of meaning capture, part of a strategically crafted argument. One way of seeing this is through the lens of the evolution of social science methods and how the shift from determinism to probabilism already begins to undermine the definition of bureaucracy as a determinate command-and-control structure.

A. DETERMINISM AND PROBABILISM

Social science research and its policy science applications challenged deterministic and experimental models of science by using statistics and probabilities to account for events. Although probabilistic social science does not actually tell us *why* phenomena occur as they do, such models predict what will happen with a known probability of accuracy. Prediction itself is only somewhat possible, and each cause is but one variable among other variables.

A notable management application of the probabilistic approach is W. E. Deming's statistical process control (SPC) (Walton, 1986), which contrasts with Taylor's deterministic scientific management. SPC is an application in manufacturing quality control. One axiom of SPC is that all production operations produce variations in the quality of product or output. SPC is a way of measuring product variations at each stage of production. Variations are charted on graphs known as control charts, enabling those responsible to examine occasions when deviations occur. A certain amount of deviation is considered common. Virtually anything can qualify as measurable outputs: clients served per fiscal quarter, duration of meetings, circumference of metal parts measured in millimeters, tonnage of potatoes delivered per truckload. An upper and lower *control* limit is set, which may be, say, one standard deviation from the mean variance. Any products that vary from the norm by more than one standard deviation would be considered abnormal, a "special" deviation that would attract immediate attention.

Deterministic quality control techniques, on the other hand, focus on flaws found by inspectors who examine the products. Whenever a flaw is found, the cause of the flaw is to be determined and corrected, the goal being zero defects (Halpin, 1966). Inspectors do not distinguish between normal and abnormal flaws, and they do not have data for evaluating the effectiveness of current management practices. It is possible that the cause of the flaw can be found, but it may not be possible to economically meet the specification for flawlessness. Unlike deterministic models, then, SPC accepts the idea of variation in a production process, although randomness is not the only contributor to normal variations. Common variations occur in association with continuous use of defective raw materials, machinery which is poorly adjusted, consistently poor worker morale, and other deficiencies traceable to systems management.

The probabilistic-deterministic distinction is evident in other management techniques, as well. Electric utility companies are often required (and this is bureaucratic in the classic sense) by state regulating commissions to employ *end-use* forecasting methods so that specific components of electricity use can be assessed. Econometric methods, on the other hand, use probabilistic statistical methods to estimate future utility demand. Only those factors which significantly account for energy demand are regarded as important in probabilistic models. (Gross domestic product, outside air temperature, regional economic growth, and regional demographic characteristics often correlate with energy demand.) The contribution of any particular end use to overall electricity demand is not worth attention unless it is statistically associated with changes in demand. Increased usage of air conditioning would be noted, but there would be little reason for utility regulators to require utilities to estimate—and grant or not grant permission to build a new energy plant based on—nonsignificant contributing factors such as rate of hair blow-dryer usage.

The distinction between determinism and probabilism may also be discerned in the relatively short history of the Environmental Protection Agency (EPA). The EPA first required industrial polluters to use the "best available technology." Thus coal-burning utility companies were required to install expensive scrubbers in their smokestacks. In this command and control mode, EPA officials were required to arrogate to themselves an expertise in the technology of pollution control for a myriad of firms and sites that they could not possibly master better than industry engineers. That form of ham-fisted government authority is yielding to a probabilistic mode that gives more discretion to site technicians. Firms are now allowed to reach targets by means of purchasing or selling pollution permits. The notion is that there is a finite amount of pollution-space, and use of that pollution-space is an expensive privilege which can be traded as if it were a valuable commodity. Firms that use too much pollution-space must purchase additional permits from firms that possess some extra pollution-space permits. The added cost to those firms that must purchase additional permits and the benefits that accrue to those firms able to sell permits represent incentives to adopt clean technology—without specifying, in heavy-handed fashion, which technology to use. By combining the concept of market incentive with probabilistic assertions regarding (a) available pollution-space and (b) a firm's contribution to air pollution, government authority appears as a mere penalty tax for a negative externality rather than as an intrusive dictator.

In another example, a marketing analyst is likely to be asked (from a deterministic point of view) a question such as: Why do consumers purchase certain products? In a stimulus-response frame of mind, the questioner assumes that purchase is the response and is curious about the stimulus because the response is worth eliciting in other situations. A different question—Who is and who is not buying product A?—will yield more meaningful data (Engel, 1968). Here the (probabilistic) questioner is interested in the properties of the individuals disposed toward purchasing product A. The properties of these individuals are probabilistically related to a disposition (to purchase). Stimuli do not deterministically cause a particular response so much as properties tend toward particular dispositions (Nachmias & Nachmias, 1988).

Many examples of probabilistic policy implementation can be adduced. A *zero tolerance* drug policy relies on command-and-control law enforcement, whereas a probabilistic drug policy would be targeted toward those drugs that are most harmful. Vice President Al Gore's (1993) *National Performance Review* proposes to "shift responsibility for workplace safety and health to employers by issuing regulations requiring self-inspections and implementing a sliding scale of incentives and penalties to ensure safety standards are met" (p. 146). The old command-and-control system, which relied heavily on on-site inspectors, has given way to a more indirect method of accountability. Similarly, determinism or command and control in budgeting has been articulated as zero-based budgeting (ZBB) and planning, programming, budgeting systems (PPBS). Probabilism settles for incremental budgeting where this year's budget correlates with last year's, a probabilistic assertion. Certain knowledge and absolute control is the fools' gold of determinist ambition.

In the next section we will show how the differences between probabilism and determinism imply different visions of bureaucracy.

B. METHODS AND THE MEANING OF BUREAUCRACY

From the standpoint of constructivism or interpretivism, views with which not every reader we hope to reach is intimately familiar, determinism and probabilism are not fundamentally different (see, e.g., Harmon & Mayer, 1986, pp. 134-155). For public administrationists trained within the mainstream of the field, however, the differences between the two open up a rift through which constructivism may be made credible. So here we show (a) how bureaucracy was historically defined in deterministic, control-conscious terms and (b) how those terms have been softened as control and rationality have given way to terms such as *satisficing, statistical significance,* or *tendencies.* The point of this genealogy is that even within standard approaches to public administration, the meaning of activities subsumed under the conflated aggregation "bureaucracy" have undergone substantial transformation.

Again, the deterministic frame implies a commitment to cause-and-effect knowledge, a belief in the presence of an objective reality, confidence that value-free inquiry is possible—that there can be a neutral distance between researcher and subject of study—and a conviction that the outcome of science ought to be the production of generalizable truth-statements or laws. (See Fox, 1980, 1990; Guba, 1985.)

Bureaucracy in the determinist conception is a closed-system model of control. A small slice of Weber's bureaucratic idealtype helps make the point:

> There is the principle of fixed and official jurisdictional areas, which are generally ordered by rules. . . . The authority to give the commands . . . is distributed in a stable way and is strictly delimited by rules concerning the coercive means, physical, sacerdotal, or otherwise, which might be placed at the disposal of officials. . . . The principles of office hierarchy and of all levels of graded authority mean a firmly ordered system of super- and subordination, in which there is supervision of the lower office by the higher ones. (Weber, 1946)

In a similar spirit Taylor intones:

> The first great advantage which scientific management has over the management of initiative and incentive is that under scientific management the initiative of the workmen—that is, their hard work, their good will, their ingenuity—is obtained practically with absolute regularity. (F. W. Taylor, 1912/1978)

The probabilistic frame represents the attempt to establish associations and correlations, a more modest project although more sophisticated in its methods. Most of contemporary mainstream social science, emphasizing statistical correlations and other measures of association, fits this category. Much of the quantitative analysis that occurs in the social sciences, such as survey research, is likewise probabilistic. In apparent abandonment of any hope for formal control, others sought to understand informal organizations (Barnard, 1938/1966) and human relations (Follett, 1924/1951; Roethlisberger & Dickson, 1939). Either way, the number of variables increased: Environmental turbulence stirred up a multitude of causes and effects, which rendered the classic bureaucratic control model inadequate.

Gradually, then, not only were the methods increasingly probabilistic, but the language, too, had moved a great distance from the absolutism embedded in Weber's description or in Taylor's promises. Terms such as *outcomes, likelihood,* and *impacts* eventually displaced the control-oriented language implicit in bureaucracy. From a probabilistic standpoint, bureaucracy was interpreted as a dysfunctional mode of operating (Merton, 1957), an ineffective procedural morass. Although control never became a moot point, probabilistic models led to a greater appreciation of complexity and indeterminacy.

Two moments are evident in the development from determinism to probabilism. Internal, so to speak, to the public administration/policy communities, bureaucracy understood as cause and effect, formal scalar command and comply, was delegitimized. The Weberian idealtype is antithetical to probabilistic insights and methodologies. From such perspective Weberian bureaucracy is the quixotic attempt to ensure certainty by way of initiating causal chains with predetermined effects. Taking the bureaucracy metaphorically as a ship at sea (as Goodsell, 1994, has most recently done) that ship was rebuilt piece by piece while at sea without changing its manifest nor destination. From the inside out, recursive patterns evolved from determinism to probabilism. That is the first moment. But, second moment, it arrives at port looking the same to those assembled to celebrate or deplore its arrival, and it bears the same name. So now (abandoning the metaphor) two traditions labor under its name. The second may correct the first, but reified names blind us to those corrections. Or those corrections may be equally or more odious, and they too can be collected under the—it can now be seen as—conflated aggregation. In this way the epithet bureaucratization collects negatives.

So what could bureaucratization mean in the context of our example about health reform? Can it possibly mean Weberian command and control? Health reform could mean such a thing if, for instance, we adopted the British model. In this case we would incorporate, nationalize, the health industry and make government employees of its members. That would be bureaucratization in the original strict scalar sense. As a rhetorical gambit cast out to a malinformed public it must surely resonate, however vaguely, as just that. "Oh my God socialized-fascist medicine with a government bureaucrat [imagined as in dark gray uniform] determining my care."

Not quite as threatening, but still potentially unsettling to those advantaged by the current health care system, would be probabilistic bureaucratization. Access to health care could be determined statistically, as has been proposed in Oregon. The probabilities of success of given procedures are articulated with one's own statistical profile. What is the ratio of costs to benefits of any particular procedure? And who gets to weigh and assign the numerical values that determine the ratio of costs to benefits? It would all be very impersonal and in that sense bureaucratic. At this moment teams of medical specialists and computer software programmers are developing a decision-tree diagnostic program to assess ailments and propose treatments. Programmed decision making feels remarkably like command and control bureaucracy to the street-level bureaucrat (physician) who wants to follow his or her instincts or try something different. "My personal physician, Dr. Kildare, would not be able to exercise his intuitive and empathetic understanding of my condition." Actually, this probabilistic model of bureaucratization seems to be where the Clinton administration is heading, as it favors managed competition (probabilism), over the Veterans' Administration model (determinism). If so, it ought to be scrutinized in terms of whether, for the sake of controlling costs, too much bottom-up policy implementation discretion will be quashed. One might also look for some mechanism (also amenable to the label bureaucracy) allowing the inclusion of equity considerations.

But bureaucracy now also means mindless red tape, goal displacement, means-ends reversals, and instrumental rationality gotten out of hand. These characteristics typify current practices in health care, and many of them do not stem in any immediate sense from government, qua government.

A constructivist point of view hugs the ground. What kind of recursive practices require adjustment? What leads to dysfunctional, irrational, and unjust delivery of health care? Is it a fragmented, private, profit-driven insurance industry that will cover only those not at risk? Is it the fear of malpractice suits that leads to testing for the unlikely? This is to say that if bureaucratization can mean so many things—from nationalization and Weberian bureaucracy, through judgments based on probabilistic-statistical inferences, to red tape—if it can mean all of these things when uttered to those unprepared to disaggregate which of these is meant—it has become a conflated aggregation destructive to rational-critical discourse.

C. SUMMING UP DECONSTRUCTING BUREAUCRACY

Formal institutions exist in the context of legitimating value orientations (efficiency, for example) that are both culture-bound and historically contingent, not at all "objective." Our habits of mind influence the way we see things. Perceptions are easily channeled and ossified when participants, analysts, or managers think that they convey something concrete, whereas the reference is actually to a shared idea—a tacitly agreed-upon set of symbols and expectations. Bureaucracy is not a neutral sign in the marketplace of ideas. Signs guide us in framing what we perceive and already imply a judgment of it. The sign bureaucracy enjoys special status in this respect because it not only is an idea in its own right, but, once reified and treated as an objective condition, it serves as a vehicle for the control and distribution of many other ideas. Yet bureaucracy quite plainly has no objective existence outside of human social interaction.

Experiencing the incoherence of bureaucracy from the inside out (i.e., from the alternating lenses of determinism and then probabilism), we are compelled to try to do better. We want to outflank the concept bureaucracy as if it were one monolithic way of influencing patterns of recursive practices. Determinist, Weberian bureaucracy would explain how some recursive practices are retained or altered: Practices are commanded, legislated, forbidden, made criminal or censurable; too, deviant behavior will result in firing, arrest, or hospitalization. But then even, or especially, Weber realized that naked power, unassisted by willing acquiescence, is not cost-effective. Thus legitimacy was proposed as power's lubricant. In our terms, power/domination requires legitimizing (reified) symbols.

Likewise, probabilism explains how some recursive practices are retained or altered. Here the trick is the manipulation of variables, rewards, tax incentives, and the like, which elicit appropriate (to the manipulators) behavior. Yet we want to argue that separately or in combination, determinism and probabilism (heretofore gathered up as bureaucracy) do not capture the evolution of recursive practices. Because both are based on *decisions* (to either command or to manipulate variables), they cannot comprehensively grasp the implementation of public policy by public administration and all of its many coconstructors of realities (Harmon, 1981, pp. 92ff). How, for instance, can one explain zeitgeist changes that occur with the change from a moderate Democratic administration to an ultraconservative Republican one in reference, say, to the enforcement of liberal programs such as affirmative action? By what conceptual means can we be allowed to recognize those shifts in attitude, the waxing and waning of zeal in policy implementation, those sea changes that affect nothing directly (no rules or laws change, SOPs remain the same), but affect everything really? We offer as an encompassing conceptualization, a metaphor if you will, energy fields.

III. The Public Sphere as Energy Field

So far in this chapter we have, first, tried to build a common vocabulary based on phenomenology, constructivism, and structuration theory. Our purpose was to show that institutions are recursive practices embedded in habitual human comportments and expectations of varying degrees of malleability. We went on to undermine the category bureaucracy with an immanent critique based on the significant shift from determinism to probabilism.

Rather then retain the category bureaucracy and aggregate the coalitions (networks, associations, task forces, cliques) with their various experiences, goals, or end visions into it, we propose instead to abandon the category bureaucracy (or strictly limit it to its original historical modernist command-control Weberian connotation). We propose to subsume under public energy fields all those activities and recursive practices currently conceived as agencies and institutions in organizational chart boxes in the bureaucracy, along with any such closely related sectors of civil society as the nonprofit social service sector, the fourth estate, and citizen groups of all kinds: all those who are engaged in activities with public implications, who are projecting actions in accordance with the implicit question, what should *we* do next?

Both determinism and probabilism presuppose the efficacy of policy design from some centralized, top of the hierarchy, point of view. A decision is made by central elites, it is then passed down to be obeyed (determinism), or it is floated like bait, to elicit appropriate behavior (probabilism). In contrast, energy fields assume a public sphere with multiple sources, like sunspots potentially flaming up from any and all points. The energy from a flame-up then pulsates out in waves of currency, affecting the field as a whole, as well as other nodes of potential flame-ups. In both the philosophical and democratic theoretical meaning of the term, ours is a radically pluralist vision.

Determinism and probabilism limit autonomous initiation of action to the apex of systems, forgetting that at every point in a system is an intelligent human being who pays attention to developments, is influenced by the news and daily events, and discusses these things with colleagues. No conceptualization of bureaucracy can explain the resonance throughout the offices of the land of, say, Anita Hill's testimony in the Clarence Thomas confirmation hearings.

Her testimony was like a sunspot that gave forth pulsating waves of energy, vectors of gathering momentum that focused conversations and dominated the water-cooler agendas in virtually every office building. The Anita Hill testimony possessed good currency. Conceptualizing de facto policy (recursive practices) adjustments as vectors of momentum and currency in energy fields can, in this postmodern age, highlight events and practices that current orthodoxies must, because of where that searchlight points, leave obscure.

We attempt for the field of public administration no less than a *paradigm shift* from bureaucracy to public energy fields, as potentially eye opening (we hope) to our field as the very similar shift from particle to wave in quantum mechanics has been for physics. In Weberian terms, we will reclaim social action from its appropriated condition as rationally organized (bureaucratized) action (Hummel, 1994). We begin with the physics story to show how a change in metaphor can change conceptualization of what is being done, which then changes recursive practices.

A. PHYSICS, METAPHORS, PHENOMENA

Again, it is well to keep in mind that institutional structures were not always as they appear in their contemporary manifestations, but were created and then modified by practice—by processes of social interaction. Physics made its appearance in historically contingent conditions that defined the domain and structure of physical science. Physics was not created whole by some primordial heroic physicist. Physics is a set of evolving recursive practices. Practice and consciousness travel apace.

Different language games orient communicators to different constellations of phenomena and codetermine them. When attention is repaid with interesting results, we seek to communicate our findings. This communication impulse is as true in child's play as it is for science. "Look what I found," we say. Physicists, finding something interesting, appropriated the category *particle* to communicate their findings in atomic research. Measurement devices such as the electromagnetic microscope, the attention of interested observers, and the categories they selected to communicate their findings became part of the phenomena they studied. In other words, the phenomena were signified with metaphors that merged with what was observed. A classic enigma is illustrative.

The double-split experiment is well-known among physicists: Imagine a panel with two slits in it, standing in front of a screen. If one of the slits is closed, light enters through the other slit, and a corresponding distribution of light can be observed on the screen. If both slits were opened, the light particles hitting the screen manifest something more peculiar in the aggregate than two distribution patterns summed. A different pattern appears, one that seems impossible if light were truly particulate. The distribution of light on the screen confirmed an alternative hypothesis based on a different metaphor: that light has the properties of a wave rather than a particle. Yet in other circumstances light was thought to be particulate. The wave/particle enigma seemed extraordinary when its implications were first perceived, and the enigma remains marvelous and peculiar. The enigma also applies, remarkably, when electrons are used instead of a source of light (Hawking, 1988).

If electrons are sent through the slits one at a time, one would expect each to pass through one slit or the other, and so behave just as if the slit it passed through were the only one there—giving a uniform distribution on the screen. In reality, however, even when the electrons are sent one at a time, the fringes (that is, the anomalous distribution patterns) still appear. Each electron, therefore, must be passing through *both* slits at the same time!

The important point was well expressed by Wallace (1989) in his discussion of quantum physics. He explained how a particle has a distinct size and location, and either bounces off other objects or penetrates through them.

Waves have three dimensions and spread out. They may pass through one another and can interact to produce interference patterns. Because waves and particles are so fundamentally distinct, it stands to reason that no object can be both . . . but electrons seem to display the qualities of both. How can we account for this?

> The enigmatic quality of this discovery may be attributed to an apparently innate tendency of the human mind known as *reification*. . . . On the basis of everyday experience, physicists assumed that the electron is a particle. This form of scientific realism, like everyday realism, ignores the critical role of the subjective instrument of observation. (Wallace, 1989, pp. 57-58)

Thus the everyday atomic particle of classical physics was reified, regarded as an independent force with material thing-ness. Certain properties were presumed to be intrinsic characteristics of the electron. But different research conditions and different measuring instruments suggested the presence of a wave. Electrons-as-particles are whole, they bounce off other particles, and they are irreducible. Electrons-as-waves merge with other waves and are infinitely divisible. Either category fails, at some point, to convey what is happening.

Additional research has added more uncertainty. Researchers working on microentities found that the type of measurement device used and the setting of the experiment seem to influence the results. Specifically, the velocity of a particle that is being measured can be measured only by disturbing it ("bombarding" it) with a minimum amount of light; hence the more accurate the measurement of speed, the less accurate is the measurement of position (Hawking, 1988). This is quantum theory's *uncertainty principle*. Social scientists may recognize a resemblance to the Hawthorne effect, in which the researcher's instrument, or the researcher herself, will produce an effect in the subject that is independent of the experimental treatment (Overman, 1991). Inevitably, what we see depends on our sensory perceptions and our instruments of measurement—and use of these tools changes what we see.

Although both the physical and social sciences are unavoidably reifying, studying human interactions entails pejorative judgments. Physical scientists observe microdynamics and name (conceive, reify, conceptualize) the electron and the proton in order to be able to communicate their understanding. When social dynamics are observed, they are named (reified) the husband and the wife or the boss and subordinate or teacher and student. The mere naming of a role brings with it expectations of behavioral compliance with recursive practices. Signifying not only communicates our understanding but normatively conditions their relationships; there is an element of prescription; judgmental aspects of an observation are only rarely bracketed. For example, when Lowi (1993) pronounces that "the assumption of selfish interests is probably the only thing on which all political scientists agree" (p. 262), he is doing more than dismissing those who would disagree (your authors among them) with the atomistic conception of the individual. He is prescribing an assumption and by doing so, in effect, insists that it be the dominant assumption about human nature. Such prescriptions are most evident when they are ill-fitting. For example, a newly appointed secretary in an academic department, trained in the private sector, cannot understand that he or she is a staffer to all, not the toady of the boss (chair). A student cannot understand that what the teacher wants is independent thought, not obsequious regurgitation.

In the final analysis, however, physicists prescribe behavior, too. Quantum theory showed that the deterministic laws of classical physics were not valid, and that the simple picture of the physical world provided by classical physics was inaccurate. Atomic particles did not behave as their laws or prescriptions indicated. Students of quantum mechanics overtly acknowledge the participation of consciousness (attention, intention, instruments of perception, conceptual categories) in the representation of physical reality (Jahn & Dunne, 1986). Particles seem like waves; waves seem to communicate among one another; the researcher influences the dynamics under study. How can these anomalous influences be taken into account? Abandoning the atomic particle as the fundamental unit of analysis was the first step.

The purpose of our excursion into physics, often thought of as the hardest or most objective of sciences, has been to show how names and metaphors influence the phenomena themselves. Phenomena, that which persons perceive, may be regarded as the nexus of three things: intentionality; something outside a person toward which that intentionality sparks (a kind of grounding for it); and a name that already entails a both judgment about what it is and expectations about appropriate recursive practices associated with it.[4] Again, we have claimed to be radical nominalists in an ontological sense; names are not the things-in-themselves. But obviously from the above analysis, names are crucial. Names for phenomena intrude to become part of the phenomenon itself. Names channel the employment of our perceptual apparatus. They allow some things to be perceived as phenomena and have the power to blinder us off to alternative perceptions, although not forever. Changing names, changing metaphors, is therefore no small niggling matter (see G. Morgan, 1986). Again, we want to say that the change from *institutions* and *bureaucracy* to *public energy field* is as important as the change from *particle* to *wave*.

It may seem overly ambitious to attempt to foment a reconceptualization of a field by a simple change of metaphor, but we work in good company. Political scientists will recall how the subfield of federalism, based on constitutional doctrine and institutional separation of powers, became the study of intergovernmental relations (IGR) (Grodzins, 1966). The metaphors, from layer cake (constitutional-institutional federalism), to marble cake (highly interactive and interdependent intergovernmental relations), and picket fences (composed of expert specialists, the pickets, held together by managerial/political specialists) (Sanford, 1967), were crucial to a paradigm shift away from institutions and toward specific program implementation. We claim, and seek to encourage, further development along lines similar to IGR, only expanding the domain of social action to gather in those interrelationships among actors/units within, between, and among agencies in addition to interested parties from civil society.

B. ELEMENTS OF THE PUBLIC ENERGY FIELD

To reconceptualize public policy and its administrative implementation as a public energy field is to remix several currents of thought. The *public* part of public energy field is the appropriation and mixing of Hannah Arendt's and Jürgen Habermas's conceptions of the public sphere. But *energy field* is a more robust and viscous term than *sphere*. Less abstract, the public energy field entails situation, context, and historicity. In the next chapter we will populate the public energy field with discursive formations. For the energy within field part, one could go back as far as the pre-Socratic Greek atomists Leucippus and Democritus (Lloyd, 1967) or Leibniz's (1646-1716) theory of a radical pluralism of monads (Russell, 1967), but fear not, we won't. It will be enough to work out a vocabulary of allied terms and suggest the dynamics of public energy fields with a policy example. Recall that this chapter has already depicted face-to-face encounters between body-subjects as the mixing of intentionalities aggregated and applied to projects. These occur in situations rife with recursive practices, which exhibit varying degrees of stability while being subject to adjustment, change, and at the extreme, abandonment. In the next chapter we want to valorize projects agonistically competing in authentic discourse. We want to say here that all of these occur within energy fields of varying—that is both expanding and contracting—levels of abstraction and scope.

A typical dictionary definition of energy is inherent power; the power of operating, whether exerted or not. Of course, energy is sometimes thought to be a strictly physical property (billiard balls colliding) even to the point of measuring electric charges of a working or dreaming brain. It is not, of course, our intention to resuscitate particle physics. Our nonphysics or even metaphorical use of the term does, though, recall the original Greek. Thus for Aristotle energy was the progressive "actualization of that which previously existed only in potentiality" (Jammer, 1967, p. 511). Adding to energy the notion of *field* connotes a space-time extension within which energy is potentially or kinetically manifest. In our use, energy field describes a phenomenological *present* or *now* charged with human intentionality. By phenomenological present/now, we do not mean a particular instant or segment of clock or calendar time. A now as an expanded present is a gathering up of sedimented comportments in *this* situation for projection into the future. An energy field is composed of bundles of human intentions, enthusiasms, purposes, and motivations projected from within varying nows.

In the social sciences, models of social interaction which would rely on *energy field* as the unit of analysis, in the place of either atomistic individuals or anthropomorphized organizations, have been encouraged by Jahn and Dunne (1986):

> Transposition to the consciousness domain of the physical concepts of electric charge and the electromagnetic field phenomena that devolve from it are also anticipated by common vernacular allusions to "charged" situations, feelings of "attraction" or "repulsion," "currents" of thought, "polarized" issues, etc. . . . Much as in physical electrodynamics, the presence of such emotional charge, with its attendant internal stress and pent-up energy, renders the consciousness susceptible to "forces," and to consequent deflections of its trajectory, that it would otherwise ignore. (p. 758)

Similarly, kindred soul Schon (1971) notes:

> Underlying every public debate and every formal conflict over policy there is a barely visible process through which issues come to awareness and ideas about them become powerful. . . . It is surprising, in the light of these considerations, how little curiosity there has been about the emergence of ideas in good currency. Ideas in good currency, as I use the term here, are ideas powerful for the formation of public policy. (pp. 123-124)

Ideas are brought into "good currency" through interaction in a particular setting with others. The ideas that circulate among participants as they interact, along with ideas generated during antecedent processes, attract participation. The energy field concept directs attention to context, that is, to substantive, robust events, and also to social interactions that constitute the sense-making process.

Accordingly, human social behavior is amenable to study using the energy field concept (compare to field theory, Lewin, 1951). Social currency circulates among people, affects their interactions, and makes aspects of recursive practices problematical and consequently amenable to change. Currents of messages to which to attend move about among human associations and social networks—in families, at the workplace, in friendship groups, in youth gangs, and between lovers. The concept of energy fields captures a more free-flowing interaction among organizational actors and environmental actors, their intentions, and the energy they bring to the field. Bureaucracy as we once knew it was separable from its environment; the energy field concept insists on radically more interdependence, even more permeability, than is granted in the open system concept of permeable boundaries. Hence organizations themselves do not have proprietary claim to energy fields because a field usually transcends both macro- and microboundaries of organizations. To the extent that participants are energized around some commonly understood and meaningful project goal, for example, that project goal displaces the organization as the unit of analysis. Parts of many overlapping energy fields will play out in any formal organization.

We will never be able to delineate energy fields with sufficient specificity to satisfy a policy analyst trained in microeconomics. We will never satisfy those committed to positivist protocols of science. Energy fields invite *interpretations* and interpretations are themselves part of an energy field. Instead of being true or false, interpretations will have only as much currency as they can gather up from the curiosity-charged intentionalities which they reach and engage. They will themselves be charged poles of an agonistic discourse. There is no God's-eye standpoint from which a priori standards of valid interpretation can be promulgated. But, again, energy fields opens up avenues of interpretation unavailable to top-down, bureaucratic command and control policy implementation. An instance is presidential power/influence.

A formal organizational conception of presidential power is straightforward. At the apex of a huge multiagency bureaucracy, the president should be able to say to his cabinet: "I want such and such done." This message would then be translated into a command attached to a rule or set of rules, then to be passed down through the chain of command until at the last rank separating the bureaucracy from the population, it is implemented by line personnel. This is deterministic billiard ball implementation. Of course, no one thinks it is that simple, but that is the base ideal around which both prescriptive and descriptive policy analyses are clustered (see Fox, 1990). Suppose instead, we start with energy fields. Viewed this way, the presidency is an important gathering place for intentionalities, possessed of political and social currencies, having been gathered up from recent nows, conducted (with entropic losses) by recursive practices of an energy transformation node. These currencies reverberate out along various vectors of momentum after passing through the transformer. The subsequent receptors, capable of renewing or depleting the flow of energy, include not only the descending ranks of department, agency, and unit executives, but all humans independently, or more likely in groups and cliques, to whose life projects these vectors of momentum are meaningful. Presidencies gain or lose influence when they, as transformation nodes, gain or lose capacity to either gather and aggregate from the environment sufficient currency to be meaningfully transformed, its ability to transform it, or its ability to conduct it. Put another way, a presidency stands or falls on its ability to transform and conduct currency and thereby generate vectors of momentum that will become meaningful—that is, will possess social currency—for others.

Now then, consider that a presidency is but one transformational node, albeit sometimes the most important one, in a public energy field. As but one node among many in an energy field, it has no real fixed physical position as naive sender-message-receiver (S-M-R) information theory would have it. It may be the receptor for other transformation nodes in three-dimensional kaleidoscopically shifting configurations. The energy field may be so charged as to cause leakage in conduction (e.g., insurance companies conduct a countercharge against Clinton's health care plan). This last analogy, leakage in conduction, may be used to interpret the current admonition about the Clinton administration: Stay focused on one thing at a time; capture the momentum vectors and supercharge but one sector of the public energy field at a time. Clinton, elected by plurality, does not have sufficient currency to do more than one thing. Only the lack of imagination, space, and reader patience prevents endless articulations of similar examples. We want here only to set up the possibility of energy fields as the arena in which a democratic pluralism of discourse formations may gather up and then augment or deplete other currencies in response to the question: What should we do next?

We do not think of ourselves as original philosophers or thinkers building new landmarks in intellectual history. What this chapter has tried to do is synthetic, not analytic in the sense of the meticulous architecture of position building. To bury orthodoxy and to avoid the pitfalls of the postmodern condition, public administration needs a new model to which to aspire. For that we offer the discourse model. To assert itself such a model needs the latest and most sophisticated underpinnings that social theory can furnish. Phenomenology as base to constructivism, the two combined as base to structuration theory, and the three combined as base to energy fields has been our attempt to provide it.

A phenomenological base avoids the pitfalls of foundationalism. We have appealed to no universal or essential first principle. We need make no claim about the nature of the ontologically "real." We start only with the proposition that body-subjects find themselves in situations in which their intentionalities find fruition. Those situations include alter egos with whom we conspire to give, as well as appropriate, meanings (but no fixed prior meaning).

The concept of embodied subjectivity, however, does imply a way to subtend incommensurability and neotribalism. The symbolic meanings of particular language games may indeed grow apart and become incommensurable. But body-subjects cannot be incommensurable in the same sense because of the extensive band of similarity between the bodily comportments of otherwise divergent humans; irreducible incommensurability can occur only between Cartesian contemplative consciousness. We may not use the same word to say "cold," but we recognize in body-subjects like ours that stiff, brisk, stoop-shouldered, taut-ribbed walk to the nearest shelter during the winter months. Alternatively socialized body-subjects will in common retch at the scene of mutilated bodies at a crash site.

Our use of structuration theory and public energy fields implies no canon. Recursive practices can be Eurocentric, or not; patronymically gender-dominated, or not; or elitist or egalitarian. The recursive practices of a constitutionally founded institution are not in principle favored over the recursive practices of a central-city gang. Moreover, a public energy field can be positively or negatively charged in many ways by many types of participants and ways of participating.

We must leave to the next chapter the task of proposing a way around postmodern hyperreality. We will propose nodes or enclaves of discursive social formations.

Notes

1. We classify ourselves somewhat reluctantly, but rather we do it ourselves than be assigned a box by someone else. What we develop here is consistent with what is known as constructivism, but goes beyond it. Constructivism, which stems from Berger and Luckmann, does have a phenomenological base as we do. There is, however, a difference. By assimilating the phenomenology of Merleau-Ponty, as opposed to that of Schutz, we are able to better account for the body-subject in situations than Berger and Luckmann do. Furthermore, by tacking on the innovations of Giddens we are better able to account for what people take to be institutions than constructivism can.

2. Husserl scholars generally consider the mature elucidation of intentionality to be contained in Husserl (1962, pp. 235-349). For short renditions of intentionality designed to prepare readers for Merleau-Ponty's innovations see Langan (1966, p. 18) or Kwant (1963, pp. 156-157).

3. The plunge into idealism is attributed to Husserl's introduction of the superordinate realm of the transcendental ego. It is the controversy surrounding the transcendental ego which loosely divides phenomenology into two camps, transcendental phenomenology and existential phenomenology. Husserl and, especially important for American social science, Alfred Schutz belong to the former, whereas Merleau-Ponty, Heidegger, and the French phenomenologists belong to the latter. A concise review essay of these issues is Edie (1967, pp. 237-251).

4. Technically a phenomenon is a human perception that is the conjoining of noema (intentional spark) and noemata (the object); see Fox (1980).

5 Warrants for Discourse

We have argued that the representative democratic accountability feedback loop is neither representative, democratic, nor accountable. Even if it were any of those things, it only imperfectly "delivers" policy to "targets" through the proliferation of ever more layers of lawyerly rules. Moreover, chains of command within closed, hard-bounded agencies and bureaus are only rarely the effective mechanism for policy articulation and change. Nor are they in any way to be preferred by any workable democratic ideal. Policy happens, we have contended, by way of vectors of momentum that are not contained, not superconducted, by institutional structures. Currents of policy sweep through and alter recursive practices by altering the meanings socially constructed by groups of humans. Thus we claim that the formation, implementation, and administration of public policy may be better grasped as energy fields populated by nodes of intersecting human intentionalities loosely organized around problematics—questions of what we should do next. If our claims are convincing, benign means of initiating, transforming, and actualizing momentum vectors require theorizing. That is the task of this chapter. A well-wrought theory will, in turn, bring new light to practices that were heretofore opaque. Properly theorized, positive aspects of those practices may be valorized for affirmation and destructive ones identified for abandonment. That is the task of Chapter 6.

As we have suggested more than once, we propose a discourse theory of policy and its administration. We proceed in this chapter to first appropriate the policy perspective of Deborah Stone to depict public policy as a struggle for meaning capture. Second, we explicate the contributions of Jürgen Habermas and Hannah Arendt to the discourse theory we adopt. Third, we display the tacit procedures for authentic discourse, the warrants for discourse.

Fourth, we argue against potential critiques, that our discourse theory is a set of recursive practices that are as democratic as can be hoped for in the postmodern condition.

I. Policy as the Struggle for Meaning Capture

Public policy is not the result of a purely rational discovery of objective Truth to which governments then respond with solutions infallibly deduced from that Truth. Although such a truism seems self-evident to a field that has traversed from rational comprehensive assumptions to satisficing, probabilism, and incrementalism, it is possible to argue that we have not traveled far enough away from the chimera of objective Truth. This, indeed, is the burden of the relatively recent work of Deborah Stone's *Policy Paradox and Political Reason* (1988). She points out that policy discourse is inherently political. Her book is a response to dissatisfaction with policy analysis that is excessively rationalistic, objectivist, and dominated by economics and its paradigmatic accoutrements: individualism, exchanges, and markets. Her conceptualization of the "strategically crafted argument" helps the argument being made here most directly by distinguishing between political reason, on the one hand, and rationalistic analysis based on the utility-maximizing, atomistic individual, on the other. She further notes that policy dialogue occurs within a political community that does not resemble the economic marketplace, but the polis.

The mainstream bias toward rationalistic objectivist policy analysis would lead us to believe that there is a single truth that can be found out about policies. For Stone, policies are paradoxes wherein several contradictory truths may simultaneously exist, depending on one's point of view. This is because policy disputes are instances of political reasoning, not some abstract logical calculus with discrete, fixed-meaning, invariant units. Political reasoning proceeds by metaphor and analogy, and discourse participants try to persuade each other that some problem or solution is like one thing rather than like another thing.

> Shared meanings motivate people to action and meld individual striving into collective action. Ideas are at the center of all political conflict. Policy making, in turn, is a constant struggle over the criteria for classification, the boundaries of categories, and the definition of ideals that guide the way people behave. (Stone, 1988, p. 7)

It follows that not science but the clash of metaphors, similes, and analogies, strategically crafted arguments, and rhetorical gambits are the actual determinants of policy. Indeed, invoking scientific jargon is itself a rhetorical gambit and part of a strategically crafted argument. The game is not about truth but about meaning capture; truths are won, not found. Again, as per our constructivist underpinnings and consistent with Stone, a successful policy will change recursive practices, those reiterative patterns of conduct that constitute our cultural habits and assumptions. Recursive practices can at bottom be changed only by changing human intentionalities and interpretations or by eliminating the humans who have them, by massive reductions in force (rifs). Coercion is, of course, one way to change those intentionalities. "Do what the boss says or you will not have a job" is a powerful argument. But soon, those persuaded by such means will no longer exercise autonomous intentionality on behalf of the situation. The situation will no longer be theirs. They will simply plod along, bodies no longer activated by their own conscious perceptions. Their active intentionalities will find alternative venues: daydreaming, clock watching and time serving. But we are now told by cascades of pop-organizational-business books that our organizations can no longer compete without the active intentionalities of all participants. That introduces the need for all policy, all changes in recursive practices, to have at least the manipulative appearance of having discursive elements. As Weber long ago recognized, legitimacy is more important than raw power. Policy legitimacy would seem to require participation. If, as we say, legitimacy no longer attends to the truncated participation allowed by the loop model, discursive ways to attain it seem desirable.

Now although Stone's polis model of the clash of strategically crafted arguments implies discourse, it need be neither a democratic nor an authentic one. Under postmodern conditions, exclusion from the discourse occurs in undemocratic ways. Access to the public airwaves is restricted to those who control the media organizations or those who can purchase the advertising; the result is not an elevated conversation, but the clash of self-referentially epiphenomenal symbols. As we write, the struggle for health care reform traffics in such slogans as "bureaucrats choosing your doctor," "health care crisis," "no health care crisis." Strategically crafted arguments, metaphors, rhetorical formula abound, but they rarely meet in authentic conversation. They float past one another in a hyperspace cluttered by the debris of short-lived logos. These were attempts of self-interest groups to influence public opinion with vacuous slogans and thereby inauthentically influence elected legislators to make self-interested interventions to skew more authentic deliberations. Meanwhile, underneath these, a more authentic discourse among so-called "wonks" of all ideological stripes occurs. Here too there are metaphors, strategically crafted arguments, and rhetorical gambits to capture meaning. But here they engage one another. Here the metaphors are single payer, managed competition, regressive taxation, governmental provision of minimums, the Prudential insurance model of just distribution of health care resources, rationing, triage, and the like. We need a way to be able to say that the latter type of struggle for meaning capture is more authentic than the former. Its authenticity is in turn based on its adherence to certain democratic norms, captured we believe by Arendtian and Habermasian discourse theory, translated by us as *warrants for discourse.*

Two aspects of discourse philosophy need to be captured before our own appropriation to American public policy/administration is accomplished: authenticity and agonistic tension. For the first we turn to Habermas. Hannah Arendt will help us with the second.

II. Authenticity, Ideal Speech, Agonistic Tension

Both Habermas and Arendt have been concerned in different ways with theorizing a public sphere wherein autonomous political will formation might occur independent of either the state apparatus or the economy (compare Villa, 1992). We must quickly say that our underpinnings in constructivism and structuration theory forbid categorizing lifeworld practices in such grand metanarrative spheres. Having already decried the blindering effects of reified stable institutions and the bureaucracy, we are not about to cop out to even more abstract categories. To do so would entail conceiving public administrators as agents of the state, whereas, as will be shown, we prefer that they be granted warrants for discourse. Nor do we think that the economy can be fruitfully conceptualized as some autonomous force of Hegelian proportion. What we seek to borrow from these social theorists, instead, are minimum standards for a normative theory of discourse. Not discourse in some one monolithic sphere, but multiple overlapping discourses as nodes of activity and currency enrichment in energy fields. Despite these reservations, one wants desperately to figure out a way to affirm a public policy process that is critical and deliberative in Habermasian (Calhoun, 1992, p. 17) and Arendtian (Honig, 1992, p. 226) senses; something more than the mobilization of bias (Schattschneider, 1960), the aggregation of prejudices, and the fomenting of fear. We turn first to Habermas's project of developing an emancipatory ideal based on speech acts.

Habermas (1975) writes from the Frankfurt School critical theory tradition, the project of which was the critique of domination. Beginning with a priori egalitarian principles, critical theory worked to reveal overt and subtle manifestations of fundamentally irrational enslavements of humankind. They sought to reveal domination on grounds that recognition is prelude to transcendence. Especially subject to critique was the arrogance of the Enlightenment and its offspring: science and rationality and the dominant culture and belief system of which these are important parts. Taken together these are considered to be an ideology. By the Frankfurt definition, an ideology is a worldview that justifies the existing but fundamentally alterable power structure. Such ideology presents itself as "natural," "objective," and "neutral." Marcuse (1964) called it second nature, because these are aspects of our social being that appear as simply given rather than as partially true or true only until we decide to change them. The error is in taking what is variable for a constant. An already explicated example of such ideology would be the belief that hierarchy is in the natural order of things. If natural, it cannot be challenged, nor can we do without it. If, conversely, hierarchy is only a transitory truth, it can be abolished, negated, transcended, and overcome.

Frankfurt School philosophers have sought to confute ideologies of domination (capitalism, scientism, technicism, bureaucracy) that constrain (what they take to be) fundamental human equality from asserting itself. Habermas's theory of communicative competence is one such attempt, and this one is unique in that he takes up the challenge of establishing the superiority of his own truth claims over the ideologies he and his colleagues at the Frankfurt School were criticizing. Without such grounding, it had become clear, defenders of status quo ideology could simply reply to Frankfurt School charges: "Same to you!" Even if conservatives were to grant, for the sake of argument, the charge that theirs was ideology, there was no grounds upon which critical theorists could claim other than ideological status for their own musings.

To get past this impasse, Habermas established and has defended ever since, a claim for human emancipation from unnecessary domination based in the fundamental structures of communication itself. He interprets rationality—usually considered a modernist, Enlightenment concept—to imply any action or statement that can be adequately defended (or criticized) by those performing the action or making the statements. Habermas's rationality is also emancipatory; it requires that participants in the dialogue be essentially equal (as opposed to being exactly alike). Domination must be transcended for people to genuinely talk to one another; that is why social equality should be pursued as a matter of public policy. Freely talking to one another is essential to our being as social animals, situated as we are in webs of community relationships. Emancipation from dominating social structures is thus the *telos* or ultimate end point. Moving, as if magnetically drawn, toward such telos defines human progress. We know it because discourse, and our very sociality, require this freedom from domination. Authentic communication is thus more than a moralistic homily; it is a guiding principle on the path to human advancement.

A brief analog to traditional Marxism will perhaps be helpful to understand Habermas's innovative move. Marxists had assumed that emancipation from the domination of class society, the demise of capitalists' exploitation of the proletariat, would occur when the proletarian revolution got rid of capitalists by whatever means necessary. Then there would be only proletarians, and because everybody was of that class, no defining opposition would exist, and society would be essentially egalitarian and classless. Marxists tended to see this as an inevitable and inexorable telos of history. By the time the Frankfurt School was writing (1930s-1960s) the hope for this type of emancipation through a revolutionary working class had been dashed. In the ruins of these dashed hopes, however, lay a still very potent critique of the unjust exploitation of some by others. Habermas's innovation was to build on that critique and offer up a new emancipatory force. It is not the proletariat, the Third World, people of color, students, or any other surrogate agent of revolutionary transformation that drives us toward a more emancipated egalitarian society; it is communication itself. Communication requires equal participants. Unequal communication is oxymoronic; talk between unequals is either command or acquiescence.

The argument that Habermas lays out focuses on political expression, but it goes beyond our familiar notions of free speech. Free speech is not sufficient. Equal opportunity to engage in dialogue is also necessary. Because rational nonalienated communication is so important to our very social being, situated as we are in a web of community relationships, we have a deep and abiding interest in it. Authentic communication is the end toward which human progress is marching. Authentic communication leads to rationality, "because something is rational only if it meets the conditions necessary to forge an understanding with at least one other person" (Giddens, 1990, p. 229).

According to Habermas, a smoothly functioning language game rests on a background consensus formed from the mutual recognition of at least four different types of validity claims that are . . . involved in the exchange of speech acts: claims that the utterance is understandable, that its propositional content is true, and that the speaker is sincere in uttering it, and that it is right or appropriate for the speaker to be performing the speech act. (McCarthy, 1975, pp. xiii-xiv)

Normally these four validity claims—understandability, truth of propositional content, sincerity of speaker, and appropriateness of speech performance—are tacit or latent; they remain as background presumptions. If, however, a situation arises where one or more of the validity claims is questionable, then the discourse would shift to specifically reach accord on resolving the problem of a validity claim. At this point, the norm must be grounded somehow, or discursively redeemed. Argumentation must be reexamined so that the reasonableness of positions will out. These background presumptions are what make communication authentic, existentially speaking. In authentic discourse, we act as if we could be called upon at any time to redeem discursively the four types of validity of our utterances. Thus, in the ideal communicative arena, distortion is avoided. So it is therefore problematic when there exists a systematically distorted communication because of institutionalized inequalities. That the conditions for ideal communication are not, or are only rarely, present is the basis for a radical critique of the status quo, beyond our immediate purpose here. It is enough to say here that structures of domination systematically promote distorted communication. This can be witnessed in obsequious affirmations to hierarchical superiors and brusque commands to subordinates. To transcend this domination and bring about authentic communication, that is to allow the free play of discursive redemption of validity claims, all participants ought to have:

[1] a symmetrical distribution of chances to select and employ speech acts . . .
[2] an effective equality of chances to assume dialogue roles . . . to initiate and perpetuate discourse, to put forward, call into question, and give reasons for or against statements, explanations, interpretations and justifications . . .
[3] the same chance to express attitudes, feelings, intentions and the like, and to command, to oppose, to permit and to forbid, etc. (McCarthy, p. xvii)

Although the conditions for ideal speech are never, or only rarely, present, the ideal itself is nonetheless implicit even among conversants who have never heard of Habermas. The four validity claims (understandability, truth of propositional content, sincerity of speaker, and appropriateness of speech performance) and the assumption that fellow participants are autonomous speakers would seem to underlie any meaningful conversation. We can almost hear respected friends and colleagues deliberating. Do we not ask:

(re: understandable) Could you put that a different way?

(re: true) But is that true given that . . . ?

(re: sincerity) Are you joking?

(re: appropriateness) Sorry, you came in too late. We already covered that.

Hence authentic communication, or something like it, is a practical ideal relevant to our very sociality as human beings.

Although something like this Habermasian ideal is prologue to any adequate distinction between authentic discourse and pretenders to it, we must quickly distance ourselves from two of its aspects: its deontological character and, closely related, what we will call the assumption of harmony. As to the first, to be true to the theoretical underpinnings sketched in Chapter 4, we cannot pretend that ideal discourse has been preordained by God or any conceptual surrogates of same: nature, reason, or science. We cannot claim that the discursive ideal is to be pursued because it is metaphysically true on the basis of its own self-validating premises, for example, Habermas's contention that communication requires equality. As we translate the Habermasian ideal into warrants for discourse, we do so in an empirical/pragmatic vein. We do not propose warrants because they conform to an ideal developed in abstract philosophical thought, but because they conform to actual behaviors of humans in groups. We propose a normative but empirically based line of demarcation between a store of existing (not ideal) behaviors of body-subjects with intentionality in situations. We do assume, as does the literature around the problematic we address, that some of these recursive practices lead to democratic will formation whereas others work to abort it. And we do assume, as an a priori base, that democratic will formation is a good thing toward which to aspire. All such a priori presuppositions are, however, as our underpinnings dictate, debatable and are themselves subject to discursive redemption in agonistic struggle.

What about the normative or deontological standard at least putatively implied by the sign *authentic?* Again, there is no Platonic or ideal metaphysical form authentic against which real world approximations may be measured. Furthermore, authenticity entails integrity, but integrity implies in turn an autonomous independent self to which that integrity is consistent. If, as the postmoderns argue, selves are now decentered, there can be no thing to which integrity conforms and no way of judging, no way even of being, authentic. We have no fully satisfactory answer to this dilemma. We must simply submit as a proposition open to discursive dispute that there exists a somewhat robust, albeit philosophically and anthropologically relative, common meaning that may be socially constructed around the term *authentic*. As such authentic policy discourse is one in which discursive redemption of Habermas's background or tacit validity claims is possible and not foreclosed by relationships of superordination-subordination. Hence, authentic policy discourse is fundamentally democratic in that sense.

Closely related and second, discursive redemption in our discourse alternative for public administration need not result in consensual harmony. We do not hold as Habermas seems to do, that discursive redemption of validity claims will reach harmony and noncontroversial, nondominated consensus (Fraser, 1992). The very teleological form of the project for human emancipation presupposes, as we cannot, some foundational utopian order toward which humanity is inexorably drawn. The corrective to this presumption of metaphysical harmony can be borrowed from Hannah Arendt's (1963) more agonistic theory of discourse.

Agonistic has several connotations. *Agon* is a public competition, an olympics if you will. *Agonic* in physiology is a muscle whose contraction is controlled by another muscle. Thus there is an irreducible otherness, opposition, or tension implied in agon. But it is not a fragmenting opposition; the centrifugal opposition is held in check by centripetal commitment to common engagement. Further, there is a certain heroic characteristic to the competition. Individuals find, or rather develop, in the performance aspects of themselves heretofore dormant. *Agonic* also is used to describe a person going through internal conflict, but united by that conflict.

Incorporating an agonistic element in our discourse theory allows for a pluralism of standpoints and even a pluralism of discourses. It is expected that in an authentic discourse, the stances and views of participants will undergo alteration. Nonetheless, individual standpoints are not swallowed up by the situation to become undifferentiated homogeneous stuff. To see someone else's point and empathize with it, to understand how it is compelling for them, is not the same thing as embracing it as identical to one's own. One may endorse the provisional results of a given discourse if one has had an equal chance to influence that discourse, even if one's own points did not prevail. One can endorse without surrendering reservations one might have had and might still have. It follows that provisional answers to the question, What should we do next? will not enjoy a perfect overlap with the views of all. One can imagine a variety of agreements ranging from tentative working compromises to continue a fruitful line of inquiry all the way to the kind of mass solidarity required, for example, in the simultaneous storming of the Bastille. Answers to the question of what should we do next will occur within the space of an energy field (so to speak) with differing voltage levels to the currency, held in tension between multiple agonistic points.

With Habermas's theory in place, and having offered demurs from it based on our constructivist underpinnings and Arendtian agonistic public sphere performances, we are now positioned to offer warrants for discourse.

III. Revocable Warrants for Discourse

Habermas's counterfactual ideal, even when relieved of its metaphysical baggage and adopted as only a pragmatic standard, may be turned into a tough-minded set of criteria against which postmodern epiphenomenal codes and monologic (non)communication can be found wanting. The dampening of the American can-do spirit by public policy caught in political gridlock, the specter of neotribalistic incommensurable language games, the media framing of the news as titillation, the self-promotion of celebrity talk; these and other signatures of the current predicament lead us to this: Pure tolerance is naive, self-defeating, and disingenuous. We hold that what is (at least ex post facto) tolerable in public policy discourse is what can be discursively redeemed within the warrants for discourse. Racial epithets, sexist comments, or anti-Semitism are the language of domination and exclusion and cannot qualify as authentic communication. Public discussion that leads to public action need not abide the whole range of arguments, claims, and performances that are purely egocentric and self-regarding. Lies, half truths, and sophistry should be called by their names in authentic discourse. The uninformed opining of the otherwise apathetic should also be—and usually is—taken for what it is worth. Hired "mouthpieces" are likewise incapable of deliberative discourse lest their contract be abrogated. Human groups in the here and now actually do cancel warrants when they have been abused. The question is not will there be rules of discourse; in human groups there are always norms for inclusion and exclusion. We shun, roll our eyes, sarcastically put down, dismiss, and ignore those who violate tacit norms. We want to valorize for public policy discourses the exclusion of claims that are insincere, claims that are only self-serving, claims from those unwilling to attend to the discourse, and claims from "free riders."

In the next section we explain our four warrants for discourse, namely (a) sincerity, (b) situation-regarding intentionality, (c) willing attention, and (d) substantive contribution.

A. SINCERITY

Authentic discourse requires trust between participants. Sustained insincerity destroys trust. Therefore, discourse about serious matters, public problematics, requires that speakers strive for sincerity. We say "strive for," because even the most honorable participants in the most authentic of discourses will rarely be completely forthcoming—even to themselves. People will develop prideful fixations, will stubbornly, if unknowingly, insist on interpretations compelling only to themselves, and will screen out points that would cause them painful cognitive dissonance. Canceling warrants for ordinary human failings is not what we have in mind. Humans are probably incapable of absolute sincerity, and we cannot here define what absolute sincerity is. We can, however, (via negativa) show what insincerity is.

Making sense of the world is always a challenge. It is made more difficult when the arena of public discourse is polluted with disingenuous claims (Fox & Miller, 1993). Three somewhat overlapping and imprecise (but not exhaustive) classes of suspect claims can be identified: (a) insincere claims that betray the trust of discourse participants; (b) lame excuses for having made an insincere claim; and (c) calculated, consciously devious claims. We will not argue for censoring or outlawing insincere claims because no a priori standards are adequate to the task of identifying insincerity, and formal mechanisms for rule deployment would lead us back to the problems of· constitutional ritual. Still, insincere claims poison the discourse.

Pure tolerance is an ideal in the liberal tradition of free speech (Marcuse, 1964; Wolff, Moore, & Marcuse, 1965). Under the Millsian concept of free speech, all claims would be democratically processed and subjected to the cool scrutiny of reason where the truth will out. All claims, especially unpopular or seemingly eccentric ones, should be allowed expression on the chance that some previously ignored element of truth might turn up. But such discourse has as a precondition the sincerity of those making claims. Suppose, however, that claims offered are actually insincere. Free speech among liars is a useless gesture at best, so the question becomes how does one honor free speech and nurture it? The dominant answer has been pure tolerance: Set a good example of what the open market of ideas can achieve by tolerating equally all claims; pretend not to notice insincerity and lack of authenticity; ignore bad faith and embrace the claims so proffered as if they were premised on good faith; pretend that free speech works. We submit that, under postmodern conditions in which symbols are disingenuously appropriated in crafting strategic arguments, pretending that free speech works is in itself bad faith. Insincere claims and their accommodation poison the well from which discourse flows; by acceding to the admissibility of such claims, we collude in the occasion to manipulate others.

Insincere claims of the first kind have long been deplored. Aesop's fable "The Boy Who Cried Wolf" is the paradigm case. The moral of that story is that betrayal of trust leads to the erosion of fruitful communication. The false promises of political campaigns and inflated claims for products may be lumped into this category of insincere claims. Honest reluctance to promise "no new taxes" is debased by dishonest but emphatic claims of same. "Light" and "no cholesterol" attached to products that were always so debases claims on products actually altered for the better. Trust is lost; no one can be believed. In such a context even the sincere claims are now questionable. A common pool resource, the public conversation, has been debased.

It may be argued in any of the above examples that no one really lied: The product's lightness had not been sufficiently highlighted in the past; or, we only raised existing taxes, we did not establish new ones. Such second-order excuses debase discourse even further. Forgiveness for lying is asked by interpreting the lying as stretching the truth. Under stretching-the-truth lying may be subsumed the efforts of Bradley R. Smith, of the Institute for Historical Review and the Committee for Open Debate on the Holocaust, who suckers the purely tolerant into taking seriously the claim that the gas chambers existed, but not for the purpose of genocide. The symbols insincerely used by Smith—historical review and open debate—traffic illegitimately with the symbols of authentic discourse; we get a linguistic version of the tragedy of the commons. Overgrazing by a few on the symbols of the commons ruins its efficacy for all.

The third type of insincere claim (calculated and consciously devious) is the most destructive and the hardest to identify because it most closely mimics authentic discourse. This is no accident. Sophistry does not proclaim itself as such; its labels are hidden. We have in mind some think tank analysts, speech writers, lawyers, journalists, advertising folks, and campaign consultants, available for hire to make the most plausible case possible for themselves and/or their clients, often the rich. Distortion artists of this third kind may skew statistical indices, make elaborate justifications, and write entire and plausible books. Using subtle yet deceptive argumentation, sophists will accuse, blame, omit, gloss over, and dismiss sincere and credible arguments out-of-hand, and distort historical events that should instead obligate straightforward consideration. We think that some arguments—such as those that rationalize executive salaries by market forces that somehow exist in the

United States as in no other capitalist country—may involve the third kind of insincerity. But alas, try as we have, we cannot find grounds for a priori exclusion of potentially guileful and deceitful arguments, as we cannot know motives in advance of the utterance and cannot be sure even afterward; a claim can simultaneously be badly mistaken, yet sincerely proffered. Yet we can see the damage even as it is being done, and the result is a discourse that deteriorates; the material effect in public administration is that government is rendered impotent to act with public purpose. Government has been transmogrified into a "damn guv'ment" that is scarcely capable of protecting the public from harm inflicted by powerful private interests (Fox & Miller, 1993). Without an honest public discourse the hope for arriving at and taking action in the public interest fades.

B. SITUATION-REGARDING INTENTIONALITY

The situation-regarding component of this warrant assures that the discourse will be *about* something, about contextually situated activities. Speakers with a situation-regarding intentionality will take into account the context of the problem, the lives of those affected, and the public interest. To direct intentionality toward the problematic at hand entails the inclusion of others (because situations with public policy implications are, by definition, social) but more than that. Situation-regarding intentionality guards against the sort of abstract ideological posturing that occurs when discussants have no problematic to ponder, no situation to address, no context in which to ground their abstract theorizing. Put another way, the danger of levitating into postmodern hyperreality decreases as the concreteness of the problematic increases. By connecting their claims to a situation, discussants are better able to direct everyone's attention to the public policy question that matters most: What should we do next?

We raise the matter of intentionality to assert that one's agenda matters. Situation-regarding intentionality is the capacity to discuss matters from a standpoint that is at a higher level of generalization than the standpoint of the atomistic, utility-maximizing individual (who speaks only with a self-regarding intentionality). In transcending (but not denying) self-regarding intentionality, some conception of a public interest is called into play, even if such public interest is postulated as an ideal rather than an achievable condition. This is necessary for authentic discourse because in the case where discursive redemption is called for, it is not generally satisfactory to rely on self-interest. It would be unpersuasive to argue for a course of action in the public domain on the basis that "Course A should be pursued because it is in my own individual self-interest that it be done." This does not, of course, rule out including one's individual plight as part of a whole, nor does it rule out representing the interests and concerns of groups or classes of people as part of a whole. But these partial interests cannot take priority over the whole public interest. It should be quickly added that the matter of individual rights falls within our definition of the public interest, and so the logic of the collective does not always trump the individual (contrary to the uneasy sense we get from reading some of the communitarian literature). However, claims that reference only individual self-interest may well be overtaken by more general claims. If one were only to press for one's own interests, essentially adopting the stance of ethical egoism, and did so at every turn, there would be a tendency for other discourse participants to become wary of such claims. In time, the ethical egoist would be discounted; his or her warrant would expire.

In the Madisonian tradition, discourse is conceptualized as a debate among private interests, and there is a strong suggestion that self-interested motives do and should predominate. Narrow claims, although not explicitly encouraged, are nonetheless expected and permitted. In a challenge to this tradition, a public-regarding ideal may also be found in the literature.

> It is a kind of "we" thinking that compels individuals to reformulate their interests, purposes, norms, and plans in a mutualistic language of public goods. "I want X" must be reconceived as "X would be good for the community to which I belong"— an operation in social algebra for which not every "X" will be suitable. (Barber, 1984, p. 171)

Goodsell (1990) offers a deeper way of looking at the public interest. His argument, briefly, is that the speaker who advocates on behalf of the public interest at least claims to be decent and respectful of community norms. Other sorts of claims, such as those that occur in market exchanges, do not carry such an implication. An utterance or claim made in the name of public interest is a claim that stresses its congruity to, or bearing on, the overriding values of the relevant citizenry. The speaker is claiming to represent what the public wants and is inviting others to join the appeal using arguments broader than parochial self-interest. Participants in the discourse make meaning together, and in doing so become serious about the public interest. Those who refer to the public interest in discourse are obligated to articulate their idea of societal purpose and how that purpose should be advanced. By articulating public purpose, they make coherent the idea of public interest. Implications of an utterance must be considered; if the recommendation were put into effect, would the public interest actually be served? What matters is the meaning ascribed to *public interest* and whether the version of public interest offered possesses good currency.

C. WILLING ATTENTION

By willing attention we hope to express a spirit of vigorous, active, even passionate engagement. Willingness to perform agonistically, take chances, make mistakes, is called forth by this warrant. If entry requires at one level a shying away from the egocentric or self-aggrandizing claim, it requires at the same time a caring for the substance, process, and results of deliberation at another level. Attention means that one keeps track of events that affect particular policy discourses. Attention means also that a faithful effort is made to follow the progress of the discourse with full respect for the legitimate standpoints of others. One must listen and hear, as well as speak.

The criteria of willing attention are brought to bear in two key ways. First, lack of attention would disenfranchise participants because they would lose track of discourse progression. Those who become psychically distant from a discourse lose their ability to apprehend subtleties and nuances. Over time other participants will tire of explaining things that listeners might have been expected to grasp had they paid attention. Apathy cancels eligibility not because it is evil in itself, but because discursive competence is ultimately brought into question.

Second, participants in the discourse would rightly question the veracity of an unwilling colleague. Sharing of the discursive stage is wasted on those forced by exogenous forces to be there.

D. SUBSTANTIVE CONTRIBUTION

Warrant for discourse can also be obtained by virtue of one's proximity to the situation, by offering a unique point of view, specific expertise, generalized knowledge, or pertinent life experience, or by being able to express the concerns of groups or classes of citizens that one (actively or passively) represents. For that matter, it is a substantive contribution for one to be able to concisely summarize for newcomers the debate thus far, or to frame new categories that will move the dialogue further along. Standards here are inclusive, not exclusive, and anyone should be able to take advantage of opportunities to present argumentation in the dialogue.

It has long been acknowledged that public administrators (that is, career public servants or line policy implementers) have warrant in the discourse by virtue of substantive contribution, sometimes denigrated as expertise (see Fischer, 1990). Also, to be elected is to be invited to use warrants. To be involved in policy implementation is another invitation. To have one's values offended is an invitation. To have one's life, or the lives of friends, affected by policy is an invitation. To live and work in close proximity to the situation is another invitation. Opportunity to participate ought not depend on formal role position, institutionally determined. Those engaged in democratic discourse would welcome any and all comers who would respect the rules of discourse.

Most of us can recall instances, such as a discussion group, committee meeting, seminar, neighborhood association, or the like, where someone entered the discussion without appropriate warrant, was insincere, cavalier, or ego-tripping, was interested only in self-aggrandizement, was at the meeting only because she or he had to be, or lacked any kind of needed expertise or abilities. We can all recall occasions where the norms of authentic communication were violated. Civility or timidity probably prevented overt redemption of latent warrants. If our attempt to valorize authentic discourse has any force, and if we are right about current threats to authentic communication, perhaps civility and timidity, born of pure tolerance, need to be overcome when the now manifest warrants are violated. Speech that is insincere is useless; claims made by coerced participants should not be taken seriously; and claims made solely to maximize individual self-welfare need not command a public hearing.

This section might well have been titled "policing the discourse." But remember, this policing is done by peers, in thousands of subtle ways using thousands of nuanced clues easily picked up by competent adults. And remember that these warrants are not so much a priori as they are process norms. We do not tolerate rules that are used to automatically exclude anyone or any view. No one stands outside the door to collect warrants or signatures to loyalty-to-the-discourse oaths. People learn to be competent discourse participants in a developmental process that occurs over time and with ample opportunities to practice. We explicate discourse norms not to limit its exercise only to the purest forms, but to articulate an ideal toward which policy conversations might aspire with fruitful results. We believe that discourse may be judged a democratic process insofar as participation is not arbitrarily foreclosed to any, and all parties (obviously including public administrators) willing to abide by the very human norms of authentic discourse.

IV. Applications of Discourse

All well and good, a sympathetic reader might say, but how can this discursive ideal be a new model for public administration and policy? We hasten to admit that not every hour of every day will be spent in discursive will formation. The steady and stable delivery of public services, the utility of which has been long settled, does not require Herculean agonistic discourse. Put another way, the vast majority of recursive practices will remain as stable backdrop for those brought as figure to scrutiny.

Still, a discourse theory of public administration is normative for at least as much of phenomenological lifeworld "reality" as is orthodoxy, constitutionalism, or civism. Not every hour of every day is filled with reporting up the hierarchy to superiors, contemplating one's oath of office, or engaging citizens. All models occur (so to speak) at the edges of the massive habitual inertia of the lifeworld.

We have also claimed throughout to be relevant to both public policy and public administration. This is because we regard these expressions as identical; they refer to the same kind of phenomena. Public policy is not just what legislatures enact. Public policy is also how currency, which might indeed have been energized by a legislative enactment and given force by fiscal appropriations, is implemented at the nether horizon of face-to-face encounters (Harmon, 1981). These face-to-face encounters, the melding together of recursive practices based on a coconstructed reality, is at bottom discursive. The worksite safety inspector negotiates the remediation of unsafe worksites. The welfare intake worker negotiates a concatenation of rules to apply to a case with the agonistically inclined mother of hungry kids. The environmental regulator negotiates municipal compliance with land-fill regulations based on ambiguous rules to be applied in significantly varying locales. The prosecutor plea-bargains the majority of her cases lest the courts be even more clogged than they already are. In all of these negotiations, the better the discourse the better the policy. Sincerity, situation-regarding, willing attention, and substantive contribution are better than lying, self-aggrandizement, sullen acquiescence, and stonewalling.

Note that these instances of policy implementation are not ideally discursive, and perhaps the face-to-face encounter between taxpayer and Internal

Revenue Service auditor will never be so. The encounters are coerced, there is unequal power being applied. Governments will govern. It is still possible to claim, though, that the more the discursive ideal is approached, the more authentic the encounters will be, the less will government be "they" and the more will it be "we."

6 Nascent Forms of Discourse

We are not the first to recognize that much of public policy making takes place with very little public involvement, nor are we the first to begin thinking beyond the loop model. There are innumerable efforts to correct the inadequacies of the overhead democracy model by engaging the citizenry in direct participation. The city of Portland has gone so far as to establish an Office of Neighborhood Associations (Clary, 1986). Participation is a consistent theme in many attempts to reform the policy process; public meetings and open hearings are required by many recent legislative enactments at all levels of government. In addition to public forums, there are a variety of concepts, techniques, practices, and methods that are promoted as improvements in democratic procedures. The rubric of citizen involvement, devolution of authority, coproduction of public services, citizen empowerment, participatory research, action research, and focus groups indicates the trend, and surely there is more to come. How can their democratic potential be assessed? The answer, we argue, is by their distance from the discursive ideal described in the preceding chapter as warrants for discourse.

I. Policy Talk

There are many things that can go wrong in a discourse; the warrants are intended as a normative check against which some of the worst breaches might be identified. Cases, examples, and scenarios associated with the move to enhanced participation and democratic discourse are examined in this chapter, and a typology is advanced to critique these exemplars. We first identify several cases in which discourse resembles elite-dominated manipulation (few-talk), and then contrast this category with expressionist anarchy (many-talk). Few-talk represents the sort of politics that has frequently been critiqued by elite theorists. Many-talk represents the discursive sanctuaries that are free from elite domination. These are ultimately unsatisfactory, however, because the anarchic and disorderly structure of the discourse obviates any popular will formation or policy action. However, many-talk that is sustained over time may begin to develop structuration and coherence, the kind of authentic discourse we were hoping to find. We refer to this cast of discourse as some-talk.

Some-talk discourse describes those nascent structurations identified in the public policy literature as policy networks. The rules of authentic discourse are perceptibly in evidence in many public policy networks. Public administrators, policy experts from industry groups, policy think tanks, legislative staffs, and public interest groups, along with legislators and other kinds of citizens do try to make sense, together, of a situation. Further, they are trying to make sense of the situation as a prelude to action—there is an open question about what should be done next that energizes the participants and their interactions, creating momentum and the possibility of change.

Policy networks as such are not always ideal applications of the model—powerful participants are often able to exclude the less powerful; sometimes the policy proposals are but self-aggrandizing ploys; the arguments offered are not necessarily sincere. But the discourse model provides a set of criteria against which the authenticity of a policy conversation can be judged. Although the findings are not always encouraging, we seek to identify those forums that are intimations of authentic discourse and expose as inauthentic those that are either monologic manipulations at one end of a continuum or merely cathartic, anarchic babel at the other end.

A. MONOLOGIC MANIPULATION

The following selections are presented not because they are the best exemplars of monologic communication—TV commercials or tightly structured hierarchies would be contenders for that dubious distinction. Rather, we have included examples where participation itself was the issue—usually where efforts to expand participation were the subject of investigation. One can reasonably expect that those who study subjects such as citizen participation care deeply about democracy. But efforts to improve public input are sometimes faulted on the grounds of too much apathy, too little accessibility, too little integration of public opinion into policy, and, often, all of it happening too late in the policy process. Public hearings, as practiced, are dominated by the well-organized, the interested, and those with something directly at stake. Ironically, the result of these efforts sometimes more closely resembles a few-talk monologue than democratic discourse.

1. Few-Talk Examples

Before we initiate a critique of few-talk, what do some of these efforts at democratic participation look like? A review of the recent literature yields a range of citizen participation studies.

a. Surveys

The survey approach is frequently considered a form of democratic consultation. The one used in Auburn, Alabama (Watson, Juster, & Johnson, 1991), for instance, seems to indicate that questionnaire data gathering can be useful in making public policy, if the process is iterative (their survey is administered every April), taken seriously by policy makers, and sufficiently reiterative that participants are able to learn how to become better citizens. Indeed, Brudney and England (1982) argue that citizen survey efforts are worthwhile, although the positive effects are due to behavioral change in the citizenry as opposed to improvements in public policy. One issue that has claimants on both sides has to do with the way survey data are aggregated and then correlated. Class and demographic traits of participants are such good predictors that knowing them is, for most intents and purposes, all that is needed, according to the criticism. But Fitzgerald and Durant (1980) found that demographic characteristics such as race and income class had "surprisingly little" relationship to service satisfaction. Still others have found that responses to surveys merely reflect these very reference group norms (see Simonsen, Collins, & Barnett, 1993). Moreover, responses often amount to expressions of attitude toward government unmediated by context or situation. Finally, questionnaire responses often betray lack of knowledge among respondents about what government does (Simonsen et al., 1993).

b. Citizen Panel

Kathlene and Martin (1991) attempted to demonstrate the democratic superiority over surveys of their multifaceted *citizen panel*, which included four mail surveys, two in-home interviews, and a telephone survey. A large cross-section of the populace was invited at random to participate in the citizen panel. The point of this particular citizen panel—and the test as to whether it made a difference or not—was to measure the impact of the citizen panel project on the local Transportation Committee's publicly (and ambiguously) stated positions.

c. Policy Analysis

DeLeon's (1992) "democratized" policy analysis is an attempt to involve citizens in the formulation of public programs.

> The concept of a democratized policy analysis is relatively straightforward. Instead of involving every citizen in decision making ("or empowerment," e.g., Model Cities), the idea is to increase citizen participation in the articulation and formulation of public policy programs. Rather than having the many engage in the actual policy decision (as one finds in strong democracy), it asks that policy analysts devise and actively practice ways to recruit and include citizens' personal views into the policy formulation process. This represents a conscious effort to translate and aggregate with fidelity *individual* preferences into *public* policy. (DeLeon, 1992, p. 127; parentheses and italics in original)

d. Neighborhood Inaction

We have also considered a would-be citizen involvement effort that was not to be. Thomas (1985) documented a series of redevelopment projects in Detroit that were detrimental to residents, whose organized opposition went unheeded. Of the infamous Poletown project (in which the city's powers of eminent domain were used to clear the way for a major land purchase by General Motors Corp.), Thomas (1985) wrote:

> The real question is not why the PNC (Poletown Neighborhood Council) could not stop the project, but why it could not even manage to make minor inputs into planning the project. At no time did the city administration acknowledge the right of the opposition group to exist, much less to participate in project plans. (p. 97)

Although some question the right of the PNC to protest the project, given the economic benefits that were projected, these economic benefits were themselves debatable. So, too, were issues such as Detroit's continued dependence on the declining auto industry, costs of the project to the city, and many other related issues.

2. Strengthening Monologic Tendencies

When agencies attempt citizen participation in policy making through the use of open meetings, hearings, focus groups, or community education, the resulting policy conversation—like any struggle for meaning capture—is as likely to be prefigured as it is to be open-ended. Survey research and structured interviews are convenient examples from the social sciences of such prefiguring of the discourse. Here agents, researchers, or "facilitators" decide what issues to address, what categories are useful, what questions should be placed on the agenda. Citizen surveys may also be faulted as only "snapshots" of a dynamic reality.

> The citizen survey . . . only documents opinions and concerns at one point in time. Moreover, it is not a dynamic, interactive process—the sharing of information and ideas—between citizens and officials. . . . It is the officials who decide what type of citizen forum will be used, how much information will be provided, when in the decision process citizen participation will be elicited, and how important citizen input will be in deciding public policy. (Kathlene & Martin, 1991, p. 49)

The citizen panel, designed as an improvement, did indeed document opinion at multiple points in time, but it cannot be claimed that the citizenry was involved in a policy discourse. They filled out the questionnaire, participated in a telephone interview, and when they hung up the phone they still had no idea as to whether the elites who supposedly make use of these opinions actually listened, and if they did, what they thought the opinions expressed. Apparently, the policy activity worthy of discursive involvement happened in the Transportation Committee; citizens on the survey panel could only hope that the empaneled elites were listening.

The manipulative potential of the citizen panel is transparent when compared to the effort to expand the library, proposed separately but contemporaneously to the citizen panel (Kathlene & Martin, 1991). A failed library expansion effort had been reviewed and discussed by official oversight boards, but with little overt public participation—until the city conducted a special election. And there the expansion proposal lost. The lesson: Library advocates should have used a citizen panel. Citizen panels, if we understand this lesson properly, are necessary legitimation processes that elites must endure to have their agenda adopted, that is, to get their way. Citizen survey panels are hence properly named a "method" (p. 61); a method of manipulation, one might add.

Crosby, Kelly, and Schaefer (1986) reveal more than they intended about the problems of elite dominance of citizen surveys when they urge "the recommendations (of the citizens) should be followed." That is, they need not be. But when will they be followed? If citizen surveys make known, as they did in Dayton, a decrease in satisfaction with street cleaning, arguments for increases in street-cleaning equipment outlays are bolstered (Stipak, 1980). Citizen input will be trumpeted by those who wanted the capital equipment all along.

"Democratized" policy analysis offers the same pseudoinvolvement as citizen survey projects, which actually serve to distance citizens from direct engagement with elite policy makers. This solution, like survey research and the citizen panel exercise described above, retains the atomistic, maximizing individual as the basic unit of analysis and offers no promise that claims offered in the public arena are, or ought to be, discursively redeemed, subject to authentic deliberation, or agonistically struggled over pursuant to criteria of authentic discourse. There is no call to rise above utilitarian self-interest before entering the forum; indeed, personal preference is the only sort of claim that is acknowledged.

A point made by Stewart, Dennis, and Ely (1984) is worth remembering here. They evaluated a planning effort in Denver which "illustrates how control of important judgments in policy analysis by technical staff can limit the effectiveness of citizen participation" (p. 80). The question here is one of inclusion/exclusion and who authorized to establish the agenda. Technical staff are never neutral actors, despite the associations with terms such as objective, neutral, scientific, or analytical. Mere technicians name the categories, decide which variables are worth pursuing, ask participants to focus on one issue or set of issues hence diverting their attention from other issues. These moments of question definition are not a priori mischievous; issues must be articulated by *someone* as a prelude to social action.

Whatever the criticisms of the above faint-hearted steps in improving the public discourse, it is worth putting the criticisms into perspective by noting an example where democratic purpose was altogether absent. The citizens' struggle against the technocrats, survey researchers, and policy analysts in government staff positions for control of the agenda pales in comparison with their struggle against powerful economic interests. Detroit accommodated powerful institutions without listening to would-be participants who had a warrant to enter the discourse. Therein lies a tragedy for democracy. According to Bellone and Goerl (1992), "Not all citizens may want to participate, and they should not be forced to do so under the tenets of liberal democratic theory. However . . . there may not be enough opportunities for those who want to participate" (p. 134).

These opportunities, scarce but available, may still not amount to democratic discourse. The cases outlined above illustrate that even when the survey is designed to enhance democracy, the effect is to further strengthen the monologic tendencies of the public discourse. When elites dominate the agenda, problems of monologic discourse arise. Nonetheless, technocratic methods have increased democratization in that citizen preferences become known, and elites may now have to recognize the presence of a range of opinion dissimilar to previously expressed views. Without survey data and other forms of public input, diverse views might otherwise not be recognized. These examples may therefore be nascent forms of discourse, but whether they meet the criteria of authentic discourse is the matter to which we next turn.

3. Forfeiting Warrants in Few-Talk

With reference to those very criteria (sincerity, situation-regarding intentionality, willing attentiveness, and substantive contribution), we will next show why the citizen participation efforts described above were inadequate mechanisms for engaging the citizenry in deciding what to do next.

a. Sincerity

We have proposed the sincerity warrant to safeguard against fabrication of events and misrepresentation of others' and one's own positions. The cases above do not offer much data for assessing the veracity of claims made by any of the participants, but they do serve to clarify the grounds for misgivings:

Anonymity. Anonymity of the actual speaker is preserved when advertising agents, paid actors, or hired firms construct and deliver their persuasive messages. The same anonymity is afforded questionnaire writers, questionnaire respondents, and anonymous technocrats who code the data. Anonymity is often viewed as a virtue in social science methodology. Yet sincerity is suspect when discourse participation is anonymous; missing is the possibility of having one's claim challenged. Also lost is the opportunity to redeem one's claim to the doubters. The essential dynamic that is forfeited in few-talk is the agonistic tension that might work to create meaning. Agonistic discord implies both intentionality and social interaction, which in turn suggest the possibility for discourse. Discourse solicits a response and invites dialogue. The intentionality of participants to the discourse creates a public energy field—absent in conditions of anonymity—that may otherwise lead to social action.

b. Situation-Regarding Intentionality

We raised the matter of intentionality to assert that one's agenda matters. Situation-regarding intentionality is the capacity to discuss matters with respect to a concrete situation but in a way that references a standpoint more abstract than the atomistic, utility-maximizing individual. Some conception of a public interest is implied, even if it is postulated as an ideal rather than an achievable condition. If people were only to press for their own interests, essentially adopting the stance of ethical egoism, they would lose their warrant to participate. We do not claim to have "caught" anyone doing this, but we can see that opportunities to do so derive from the monologic character of the few-talk discourse.

Self-aggrandizement. The absence of any intervention to broaden the base of citizen input is exemplified by the Poletown incident. Those who had an obviously close proximity to the situation, and therefore an obvious warrant, were nonetheless excluded in the Poletown taking of homeowners' property. Skepticism of the intentionality should be expected when participants pursuing a particular policy goal are unwilling to have their projects discussed openly by all concerned. Who benefits from the new GM plant? When there is no opportunity to hear claims or to gain knowledge of the game being played and its stakes, the question floats freely, unanswered. There is, concomitantly, little opportunity to engage in the agonistic struggle that otherwise would lead to discursive redemption (or withdrawal) of claims (vis-à-vis the situation-regarding intentionality of the proposed action). That is, through the challenge/redemption process, it could be shown how a proposal is in the public interest, or not. The problem of self-aggrandizement is related to that of hidden agenda.

Hidden agenda. The prospects for hidden agenda increase in conditions of anonymity, although hidden agenda do not depend on anonymity. Citizen participation may be used instrumentally as a strategy of persuasion. This was explicitly acknowledged in at least two instances in the cases above. Like bogus employee participation efforts, the purpose of which is to co-opt and manipulate, few-talk citizen participation may serve a similar strategic function. Whether trying to justify a new fleet of garbage trucks, a new wing on the public library, or whatever proposal, it will help to have marshaled support by what can be fatuously passed off as citizen participation.

Legitimation of status-quo recursive practices. The citizen panel whose input was intended to advise the Transportation Board may or may not have increased citizen voice. But it had the collateral effect of legitimizing the board as the authoritative arbiter of transportation questions. Transportation decisions did not belong to the citizen participants; no action was implied by their expressed perceptions and judgments. One might conjecture the opposite, that the estrangement between the average citizen and the reins of power was accentuated. Either way, securing a power niche in the community involves quite a different set of intentionalities than does public problem solving in regard to a situation.

c. Willing Attention

Participants in the discourse may be constrained by the system of domination in which they work. Coercion being the opposite of willingness, discourse in such conditions is suspect according to the willing attention criteria. We would not be alone in suggesting that the mayor of Detroit is in some way beholden to General Motors Corporation. Could such a mayor then be expected to engage in uncoerced discourse? Power, not the better argument, is likely to prevail in recursive practices organized as systems of dominance; hence the discourse (which didn't occur in this case anyway) would be regarded as suspect on those grounds.

Aside from the possibilities of coercion (which are not likely to be problems in survey research) there is the greater problem of apathy. The time and effort needed to understand an issue in order to offer considered judgment is often not appreciated in survey approaches (Yankelovich, 1991). In survey research, ill-considered, off-the-cuff opinions—even stray pencil marks—are treated with the same solemnity as are sober judgments. It may happen that the chronically apathetic may self-select themselves out of the debate; completing questionnaires requires at least some attentiveness and some willingness. But the likelihood that respondents lack concern is accentuated by the methods of random selection. It is odd that those who demonstrably do not care one whit are given an equal chance to be selected for consultation as those who care mightily. Random selection creates circumstances that maximize the likelihood that those who do not care about the issues addressed in the questionnaire will be chosen to provide "input." Under no other selection criteria would the chances of participation be better for those who do not care. By our criteria, willing attention should be privileged, not diluted by the apathetic, nondescript masses. Tracking the argument and paying attention over time increase the likelihood, we reckon, of making substantive contributions.

d. Substantive Contribution

The people who make the substantive contribution in technocratic citizen participation are those who frame the issues—the questionnaire writers and the policy analysts who interpret the results. The bias, the articulation of issues, and the meaning capture take place in the composing, in the way they write questions and interpret results. Of course, this is why there are Democratic and Republican pollsters; no survey is neutral or objective. These are the people who articulate the controversies and structure and frame the debate. Alternatively, citizen opinion surveys may function along the same lines as does neutral competence in public administration. Elites control the direction, substantive aim, and ends of the project, while citizens/civil servants provide the legitimation/expertise. The tendency here would be to re-create status quo structurations, a tendency accentuated when elite participants remain anonymous and therefore difficult to challenge.

We have examined few-talk discourse according to the criteria of authenticity set forth earlier and have found it wanting, although not altogether condemnable. Our assessment is that it would distort the meaning of democracy to claim that the above techniques share in that ideal. We next turn to many-talk discourse, which quintessentially exemplifies expressionist anarchy.

B. EXPRESSIONIST ANARCHY

The opposite side of the few-talk coin is many-talk. When monologic discourse dominates the bureaucracies, the media, and the public conversation in general, structures for organizing and energizing nonelites are weak and ineffective. An attempt at discourse by the average citizen is like a shout in the forest or its equivalent, a letter to the editor of the local daily newspaper. Computer networks provide an appropriate metaphor for explicating the many-talk discourse.

1. Metaphor of Many-Talk

a. Computer Networks

There are thousands of bulletin boards and list servers on the so-called information highway, specializing in everthing from idle chatter, dirty words, and sexual titallation to sober scientific and philosophical deliberation. The

Internet contains a relatively serious-minded array; most bulletin boards are not intended to link up with political elites, but to communicate with others similarly situated. Those who seek the latest in erotic sex messages, mathematics, politics of the Middle East, or teaching introductory sociology will, with a bit of perseverance, find one another. These virtual communities are not bound by location, but more according to subculture, hobby, mutual fascination, and the like. Many-talk, therefore, suggests a nascent form of discourse. If sustained, it could evolve into decentered, specialized, subgrouped, and perhaps incommensurable discourses. Like-seeking likes find one another. With entire populations as pool, innumerable specialized tribes with equally specialized language games are possible.

2. Babble On

If few-talk is overly structured, many-talk lacks form at all. Like computer hackers using electronic bulletin boards, the many-talk model is mostly random bits of phraseology and unconfirmable gossip, with no situation to channel discourse. There is no object of intentionality; no "what do we do next" question that would lend itself to policy deliberation and effective action, no situation providing context to the conversations. Participating in babble, however uncoerced, deflects the prospects of collective will formation and frustrates the circulation of coherent public opinion. Many-talk has no project by which it could be aggregated as will formation. The ends of many-talk are devoured by the means; the talk itself becomes the end.

Paradoxically, the subgroupings of "like-seeking likes" may be the beginning of community. From the anarchy, network bulletin boards can sometimes forge a sort of "virtual community" to facilitate the circulation of values and public opinion. Importantly, information need not be passively received by bulletin board participants, but may be actively interpreted and commented on. Not everyone is interested in talking to everyone else about everything or nothing in particular, so subgroups form and the conversation can then sustain itself. A harbinger of some-talk begins. But before we elaborate on some-talk, a brief critique of many-talk is in order.

3. Wasting Warrants in Many-Talk

a. Sincerity

Some convention, routinization, and habituation are necessary for sustaining the sense of trust that grounds social interaction (Giddens, 1984). In normless many-talk, why trust anyone? Like the anonymous claimants in few-talk, when claims are offered by the nameless in many-talk, there is no opportunity for discursive redemption, no opportunity for a second claimant to ask, what did you mean by that? There are no accepted norms with many-talk. Otherwise recursive practices would emerge; there would be structuration and institutionalization.

b. Situation-Regarding Intentionality

With both everyone and no one participating in many-talk, it is hard to assess anyone's intention. And it is difficult to care about the undifferentiated masses even if I, too, am undifferentiated. In mass society, there are no mediating structures and the many take cues from the few who control the epiphenomenal "reality." Will formation in many-talk is not so much false as absent. Where is the focused discussion about the public thing? Where is the discussion of what we are going to do about it? When many-talk congeals to become more like some-talk, it is because a context has been given some definition, and those who are interested have something to talk about.

c. Willing Attention

The attention that is paid the discourse is freely and willingly given in many-talk—and hence, this particular warrant is fulfilled. But there is no likely field of energy which will attract any but random participants to engage in the few available forums, a sparseness attributable to the dearth of recursive practices; hence substantive, situation-regarding contributions may not be forthcoming.

d. Substantive Contribution

Substantive contributions to authentic discourse are not likely in many-talk. The nonpresence of norms, customs, and recursive practices works against many-talk yielding up substantive contributions. Even though we are inclined to think that expressing one's thoughts via a message to a bulletin board or a letter to the editor are forms of discourse preferable to, say, channel surfing on cable TV, these messages and letters would rarely create enough momentum to be considered a contribution. As with the other criteria, one can imagine a mass-society ideal where all members of society bask freely in class-conscious rapture, but such a state requires a universality that is unlikely under postmodern conditions. Although substantive contributions are possible in many-talk, the conversation is prone toward alienated communication, a simulation of a conversation, because of the lack of opportunities for anything more authentic.

Yet coherence is possible, and in the next section we will explore some cases that indicate the conditions and contexts that lend themselves to coherent policy discussion.

C. INTIMATIONS OF DISCOURSE

The many-talk category, in an ideal-typical way, captures the end of the continuum that we called expressionist anarchy, with tightly controlled, nonparticipative monologue at the other end. In practice, this anarchic sort of conversation is not sustainable; the masses of Internet users separate into subsets of topics and interests. A conversation develops about . . . something. List servers and bulletin boards on the "information highway" can be taken as metaphor for an evolving, thickening conversation that begins to show itself in the polity. At this point the conversation begins to congeal, may be sustained, and may even develop into serious policy deliberation. We call this subgrouped conversation some-talk.

1. Some Cases Evince Some-Talk

a. Bioethical Health Decisions

Efforts in Oregon to bring bioethical issues to the attention of the citizenry were originated by some concerned professionals. Hines (1986) reported on a project involving the viewing of videotapes, handing out brochures, providing speakers' bureaus, and hosting small-group and town-hall meetings to influence official bodies to pass resolutions and hence to articulate the outlines of issues in health care ethics. Hines claims that the efforts to promote the bioethical "health decisions" project had no preset policy positions. "Stands on bioethical issues are founded as purely as possible on 'the will of the people' as revealed through a broad-based process of grassroots citizen involvement" (Hines, 1986, p. 7).

b. Recycling

Another professional-initiated effort was studied by Folz and Hazlett (1991); in their example, local officials, along with a network of educators, environmentalists, and citizen groups, initiated contact with residents of city neighborhoods on the issue of recycling. The *some* of some-talk were the public administrators, educators, environmentalists, and citizen groups; they articulated the values of environmental stewardship. They were also able to rally enough enthusiasm and community attention to energize and implement the recycling program.

c. Phoenix Futures Forum

The Phoenix Futures Forum was initiated by politicians and professionals who set about to articulate a "vision statement" for the city (Hall & Weschler, 1991). Registration for the forum exceeded 700, and the event was organized to include breakout sessions, "where are we now" sessions, and topical workshops (environment, technology, transportation, financing). It is difficult to discern precisely what the Phoenix Futures Forum was, but it seemed to be about citizen involvement in producing a community vision. It seemed also to facilitate networking of community organizations and to provide policy makers with a rich source of feedback. The project had its own structure of committees and subcommittees, which sought to move the policy proposals developed during the signification stage into the implementation stage. Some participants—about 100—continue to debate what do we do next in various committees and action groups.

d. Conversation With Oregon

Simonsen et al. (1993) reported on a high-tech citizen participation effort for addressing a state budgetary crisis, the "governor's conversation with Oregon." A sample of 10,000 persistent voters was selected at random to participate in 900 two-hour exercises that combined small-group meetings with an interactive computer session with the governor. She would ask, "How well is the government spending your tax dollars?" The question was discussed locally at the various meeting sites, where educational materials were also distributed. Next, a list of services was ranked by the participants so that they could answer the next question: whether to provide fewer services, increase government efficiency, or restructure the tax system to provide more money. Discussion followed, summaries of which were presented to the governor. After the participants completed questionnaires, the exercise ended. "The conversation successfully raised issues of concern to Oregonians," according to the authors (p. 18).

e. Health Care for Poor People

Stivers (1990b) wrote about a federal program to provide family doctor-type health care in deprived urban neighborhoods and rural areas. Board members drawn from one community viewed these projects as an opportunity to help a group of people who otherwise would not have had health service. Networking methods used by board members included face-to-face interaction and going door-to-door (with donuts and a jar of instant coffee) looking for those who were interested in talking about health care.

> The community board in question was under fire from federal officials on the basis that their center was not well-managed. Two meetings between board members and administrators, however, far from reflecting a unilateral exercise of federal authority to bring the "erring" center back into line, showed that the meaning of the events in question was negotiated by both sides. . . . Community people and federal officials worked out how the public interest was to be interpreted. (Stivers, 1990b, p. 98)

In a process that, arguably, resembled authentic discourse, federal officials raised issues (identified below in italics) that board members responded to (shown in parentheses):

Only 2.5 visits a year per patient. (If we had three visits a year, what difference would that make?)

Living within budget. (Is running a deficit half the time the same as never living within our budget?)

The board does not exercise proper control. (What does the phrase "proper control" mean?)

f. Developmentally At-Risk Children

Ott (personal communication, November 1989) wrote about a program for children at risk of acquiring or manifesting developmental afflictions such as mental retardation, spina bifida, autism, or cerebral palsy. Early intervention ameliorates these ailments, allowing the children to function at higher levels later in life. Programs designed for children with these afflictions (and their families) emphasize early intervention, especially for newborns and infants in high-risk categories, to ensure that these infants and toddlers are served. However, being "at risk" is different from having a developmental disability. The catch, says Ott, is that some of the categories used to estimate risk are genetic whereas others are social/familial. "Thus, in addition to the obvious problem of government intervention in families—families whose infants do not now have developmental disabilities—there is the 'fiscal uncontrollability' factor," Ott said. In other words, there is a reluctance to fund anyone who merely might develop a disability (albeit with some known probability). Because of fiscal concerns, the preference is to serve only those identified as already having a developmental disability.

Yet, according to Ott, everyone professionally involved in this question agrees that early intervention with children who are at risk and their families is ultimately cost-effective, even if it is not within the (then) new federal funding guidelines. New guidelines followed a budget tightening, and when federal funds were drawn back, scarce state funds were often similarly (perhaps consequently) withdrawn. The professional staff members of the Division of Mental Retardation in one state were frustrated at their inability to do anything about the problem. However, at a meeting that included the main advocacy groups (the Association for the Retarded Citizens, the Law Center for People with Disabilities, Parents of Children with Down Syndrome, and the state developmental disabilities council) someone "threw out" the suggestion of "just going ahead" and serving children at high risk even though it was not within guidelines. A reluctant and risk-averse director was persuaded by his staff to consult with his counterparts from other human service agencies in the state. (Incidentally, bureau and division-level directors of human service programs had already developed a significant professional network.) Most of them backed the idea of serving the at-risk children without authorization to do so. Further, the director discovered that his own staff had already authorized services to "just a few" high-risk cases without informing him. They hadn't lied, although they had not been fully candid. They thought the need was too obvious, the benefits too high, and the costs too minimal.

The division director met with the department's chief executive officer to discuss a "hypothetical case" in which a high-risk child was provided services. The CEO expressed dismay at the new guidelines, hoped that things would not get out of hand, and preferred that he not know when and if ineligible clients received services. The division director then informed his counterparts in his bureau-chief network, as well as the heads of advocacy groups, that the division "might" start approving funding for services for "a few truly high risk very young children." Serving too many was informally forbidden, as was claiming these services as a right. If anyone "blew the whistle" the policy would be finished, and lying—if the higher-ups asked— was out of the question.

2. Some-Talk Possibilities and Problems

Some intriguing issues are apparent in the some-talk abstracts rehearsed above. Regarding Oregon's health decisions project on bioethical issues, by accepting Hines's (1986) seemingly exotic claim that there was no "preset policy position," we can view this policy effort as consequential meaning-making activity; that is, having elements of authentic discourse. Articulating the outlines of the difficult ethical issues—such as when and whether to "pull the plug" on expensive technology that sometimes only prolongs suffering without improving the quality of life— was a substantive contribution from those health care professionals who brought their proximity to the situation to bear on behalf of the public conversation. The process may also have contributed to collective will formation for Oregon's vanguard health policy proposals.

Although the recycling program seemed to rally the community, this project has a familiar theme. The message is: If you really want to control their behavior, get them involved in the process. Neighbors who were expected to "coproduce" recycling by sorting their garbage were brought into the process for instrumental reasons, not to decide what to do about landfill problems. In addition, the recycling program is a fragmentary policy re-sponse that avoids challenging institutionalized practices. The program started and the discussion ended before wasteful commercial packaging practices or consumer excesses could be included in the discussion. It is an incomplete form of policy discourse, limited in that it was not sustained long enough to initiate an authentic discourse on the waste disposal/waste creation problem.

The governor's conversation with Oregon was an incomplete process, too, and the public dialogue that had been initiated was all for naught, as the governor and the legislature began bickering over the timing of a planned budget referendum. Simonsen et al. (1993) provide their own interpretations of what went wrong, but it seems to us that the problematic structural feature of the governor's policy defeat was in sending the proposal to a plebiscitary and essentially monologic arena (i.e., the public referendum). The bureaucrat bashers' monologue had already captured meaning there, and a warrant for authentic discourse is irrelevant to those who want keenly to foment oppo-sition to government. Nonetheless, the governor's conversation stands as a nascently innovative form of public discourse.

In the neighborhood health clinic example, even though the exchanges were essentially two-party (agency and board), with the agency in the dominant position, the deliberations revealed an agonistic struggle over meanings and interpretations. The outreach effort, symbolized by donuts and instant coffee, shows the face-to-face, human-scale interaction that energized a field of forces extending across any would-be organizational boundaries.

The human service professionals who wanted to serve developmentally at-risk children were narrowly drawn, mostly from the ranks of human service professionals, opening the way for the public-choice-style complaint about bureaucratic aggrandizement. Some-talk will always be limited to those who express willing attention, however. So when the policy involves spending money from the taxpayers at large, the political tensions are predictable.

Without being ideal, the examples above, taken together, show that some-talk yields strong possibilities for a democratic discourse. Participation in some-talk is not a one-time discussion, but is sustained over some period of time. A sustained, two-way conversation may explain why some-talk fares better with respect to authentic discourse than either few-talk or many-talk.

3. Redeeming Warrants in Some-Talk

a. Sincerity

With a sustained conversation, participants develop reputations among discussants regarding the quality of their claims. In conditions of recurring interaction, anonymity provides no protection for the disingenuous. The recycling discussion was, among the cases discussed, the least well-sustained conversation.

b. Situation-Regarding Intentionality

In the cases described above, the issue on the table was not what's in it for me. Whether the issue was a better Phoenix, bioethics, or care for developmentally at-risk children, the "what should we do next" question was framed at a level of abstraction above rational self-interest, yet with respect to concrete problems. Unlike the iterative survey in Auburn, the discussions were inspired by an occasion or series of events, rather than by the yearly calendar cycle, a purely arbitrary and ritualistic scheduling of public discourse. There were concrete problems to discuss. In few-talk, we did find well-defined concrete problems, but they were so well-defined that citizen input was reactive to predetermined categories of understanding. Because the participation in the some-talk discussion was inclusive (even in the case of the developmentally at-risk children, an advisory group was involved), there was a public-regarding check on the process.

In the developmentally at-risk case, the situation was quite difficult. Human service and health care professionals were trying to decide what to do in the implementation stage of a policy, and the rules made the issue a difficult one to discuss openly. After all, there are rules against violating rules. However, their closeness to the situation was their overriding warrant. Follett's (1926/1978) wise advice "to unite all concerned in a study of the situation, to discover the law of the situation and obey that" (p. 33) was heeded in this instance. Heclo put it a bit differently, but also emphasized the importance of being well-informed and understanding the context:

> The price of buying into one or another issue network is watching, reading, talking about, and trying to act on particular policy problems. Powerful interest groups can be found represented in networks but so too can individuals in or out of government who have a reputation for being knowledgeable. Particular professions may be prominent, but the true experts in the networks are those who are issue-skilled (that is well-informed about the ins and outs of a particular policy debate) regardless of formal professional training. More than mere technical experts, network people are policy activists who know each other through the issues. (Heclo, 1978, pp. 102-103)

Two additional interpretations of the developmentally at-risk children case merit further consideration. One, from a rational, self-interested frame of reference, is that bureaucrats are once again expanding domain, increasing service levels beyond that which the public wants, all the while keeping themselves busy and in demand. This is essentially the public choice interpretation, which assumes that bureaucrats, including those who work in the helping professions, are motivated to act on the basis of rational self-interest. And indeed, self-aggrandizement implies that the intentionality of the participant is not oriented toward the situation, or the context at hand.

A second interpretation is along the lines of M. P. Follett's "law of the situation." This interpretation serves as something of an antidote to the unrelenting suspicion that bureaucrats are in it for themselves (and only for themselves). She wrote that

> the people do live, do carry on their activities from day to day, and all that the advocates of democracy want is that this shall be recognized in its full significance. Democracy is a denial of dualism in every sense; it is an assertion that the people who do the doing are also thereby doing the thinking, that a divorce from these two is impossible. (Follett, 1924/1951, p. 203)

Thus Follett urges deference to the activity, the context of relations from which the collective will arises. She rejects the notion that the collective will is a collection of individual wills or economic preferences. Rejection of those atomistic conceptualizations begins "when we began to observe that the joining of men's wills always took place *in reference to* a situation, when we saw that we were always studying, not men's 'minds,' but their activities in reference to a situation" (Follett, 1924/1951, p. 207). Hence, if we are to reference the situation that the mental health staff found themselves in, their actions are redeemable at the least, perhaps even brave.

c. Willing Attention

Participation in some-talk was often associated with job-related responsibilities, unlike participation in few-talk or many-talk. As described above, active involvement in the situation also entails willing attention. The Phoenix Futures Forum started with 700 registrants at the opening forum in 1988, but 2 years later there were 100 "action committee" members[1] (Hall & Weschler, 1991). The fact that 600 people migrated out of the conversation does not in itself diminish the vitality of the discourse or the public spiritedness of the 100 who persevered, but it does suggest that willing attention is difficult to sustain.

d. Substantive Contribution

One of the important contributions in the above cases was to facilitate a public articulation of an issue. This was true for the bioethics case, the Phoenix case, and the governor's conversation. And in the case of developmentally at-risk children, there was a conversation oriented toward resolving the question of what should we do next. Although this conversation was less open than the others, the peer group did not have to suffer fools and free riders; they avoided this by implicitly enforcing the substantive contribution warrant.

In sum, then, some-talk is preferred over few-talk and many-talk. Its context-specific discourse and unwillingness to suffer fools and free riders narrows participation somewhat, but the enhancement of situation-regarding intentionality and sincerity vastly outweighs that fault. The categories we have been using include few-talk (monologic manipulation), many-talk (leading to expressionist anarchy), and some-talk. Of these, some-talk intimates the kind of discourse we have in mind, although participation tends to be limited de facto (but not de jure).

We should wonder about the political debate that is allowed to proceed on the basis of rational self-interest (using atomistic individuals—such as those who fill out survey questionnaires—as the unit of analysis) or whether a more situation-regarding warrant is needed, one in which *self* yields its primacy to *we-who-face-the-situation.* Those who pursue policy agenda in the collective arena must be willing to substitute such self-regarding intentionality with a situation-regarding intentionality.

We have not "proved" the veracity of our discourse theory in a way that forecloses all competing interpretations, but we hope we have demonstrated the reasonableness of our approach. Intimations of authentic discourse may be found even among those who are not self-consciously trying to improve the functioning of democracy. The some-talk discourse is in many ways analogous to what has been described in the policy literature as policy networks. By network, we refer to social relations that are recurring and have momentum, but are less formal and bounded than social relations institutionalized through organizational roles. Network relations are sufficiently regular that sense making, trust building, or value sharing may occur. Policy networks are those sets of relationships in which participants aim their activities toward some collective project or purposive action.

II. Some-Talk in Policy Networks

Policy networks provide a way of processing dissension and conducting some-talk conversation. The attention of many people, possessing diverse knowledge, interests, and experience, is focused on a limited range of policy possibilities. These possibilities are charged with intentionality in a public energy field of forces, interests, and voices. The process of listening, speaking, and reciprocal persuasion may change views, adjust expectations, or create new capacities for action. Many putative attempts to involve citizens lack important aspects of authentic discourse; efforts to involve the citizenry in governance were often found to be wanting. We try, in this section, to announce these ill-fated versions of policy networks, which serve as warning for those pursuing a democracy defined in terms of authentic discourse.

Yet we would not suggest the possibility of discursive democracy were there not likely instances of it. Networks of publicly interested discourse which transcend hierarchical institutions provide a feasible model for public administration. Some policy networks, interagency consortia, and community task forces exhibit potential for discourse. In these nascent forms are found think tank experts, legislative staff, policy analysts, public administrators, interested citizens, process generalists, even elected officials participating together to work out possibilities for what to do next. There are occasions where meaningful, situation-regarding discourse occurs.

The concept of policy network captures aspects of American government ignored by other approaches. Powell (1990) contends that the network form is a third type of social structure, distinct from either market or hierarchy forms, a typology first developed by Williamson (1975). Granovetter (1985) argues that networks of social relations produce trust that is otherwise lacking in both the market and the hierarchy. He argued further that social networks reduce pressures for vertical integration (that is, interaction-intense networks can possibly displace hierarchical institutional structures without a reduction in coordinative capacity), a proposition that has interesting possibilities for a nonhierarchical public administration should the network model and discourse theory prove useful.

The advantage for public administrationists studying discourse in policy networks is that important dynamics, especially policy activities that span organizational boundaries, can be subject to investigation, rather than condemnation as thefts of sovereignty by overzealous bureaucrats. The danger here is that the "iron triangle" framework makes all networks show up as subgovernments confiscating democracy from the legitimate sovereign. That is what appears on the radar screen when policy networks are viewed through the lens of orthodoxy. We want to look at policy networks using the lens of discourse theory, but this does not make the problems disappear. Even the purest of discourses has winners and losers. Investigations inevitably show resources, power, and influence that are unequally distributed, the presence of shifting coalitions with one of them likely to dominate, and struggles by the nondominant actors for a different arrangement (Keller, 1984; Wamsley, 1985). These sobering considerations of power and inequality suggest the need to differentiate networks that hint at authentic discourse from those that do not.

A. NONDISCURSIVE POLICY NETWORKS

There are various forms of extant policy networks; some do and some do not display potential as a forum for authentic discourse. One form of policy network that is worrisome to many who have considered the subject is the form that is dominated by one or a few powerful institutional actors interested in stability and procedural regularity, termed *corporatism* by Kaufmann (1991b). Another network form worth investigating is the in many ways idyllic local community whose members live in solidarity with one another; the downside of this community is its provincialism. A dark, antidemocratic underbelly also attends the communitarian notion of community; among the problems are oligarchy, reification, the regarding of entities as citizens, and the problem of intrusive fussbudgets. These matters will be taken up in the next sections. We begin with the problem of corporatism.

1. Corporatism

Corporatist policy networks are characterized by mutual dependence developed historically through agreements and negotiated mutual understandings. One would be hard-pressed to draw meaningful distinctions between corporatist policy networks, iron triangles, and the subgovernments that Lowi (1969) has lamented. Administration is becoming accountable to groups and experts, not the public at large, he fears. Whether a policy network exhibits these characteristics or not is an empirical question, but even here the data are focused by the lens one is peering through. Through the orthodox loop-model lens, one sees illegitimate cabals confiscating the public's domain. Other lenses, such as the one used in Miller's (1994) environmental policy network, show that there is a continuum along which subgovernments and policy networks run that varies from public regarding to narrow-interest regarding. Corporatist networks are located at the narrow interest-regarding pole.

Participants in the corporatist network—typically representative of corporate entities or agencies—withdraw only at high cost to their home organizations because the network is imbued with precedent, procedural rule, and previously worked-out arrangements to which the various participants have adapted. Public administrators who work with regulated industries or long-term suppliers/contractors are likely to interact with representatives of corporations in this sort of bargaining network. Whether the specific issues revolve around prices or rates (as in a monopoly industry), protection of the public from harm (as in manufacturing or food processing industries), allocation of scarce public goods (such as radio airwave bands), or in long-term procurements (as in the defense industry), the public administrator will be tempted to settle into a comfortable and enduring relationship based not on value consensus but on procedural agreement. Interlopers to the process—perhaps an upstart company or a citizen action group that seeks to challenge the agreement—are dealt with ruthlessly, according to Kaufmann (1991b, p. 228). Procedure- and precedent-oriented corporatist networks do not necessarily enjoy a calm environment, however, and diverse interests are sometimes, given the appropriate window of opportunity (Kingdon, 1984), able to break in.

In reporting on changes in the policy process in Britain, Smith (1991) notes that at one time, food policy was negotiated within such a corporatist community. A highly publicized report on salmonella poisoning burst the closed boundaries of this corporatist network. Now, not only agribusiness, but also environmentalists, consumer groups, nutritionists, the Ministry of Consumer Affairs, retailers, food manufacturers, and university scientists have taken an interest and participate in policy discourse. This exception—the opening up of a corporatist network—makes our point. Corporatist networks are notoriously exclusive because smooth patterns of interaction are preferred (Kaufmann, 1991b). And this exclusiveness lessens the chance that competing claims can be offered. Closed-network participants are thereby not called upon to discursively redeem claims that might be challenged, were discursive warrants more widely spread. But lurking beneath the surface of the procedures lie substantive issues where stakes (often profits) are compelling and open discourse is risky. The authenticity of the corporatist discourse is questionable to the extent that self-interest crowds out situation-regarding intentionalities.

Corporatist networks thus share the discursive shortcoming elucidated in few-talk, but corporatism is not the only network form that presents problems.

2. Community of Provincials

Solidarity is a term used by Kaufmann (1991a) to refer to a form of coordination of public activities which characterized traditional societies. More generically, Gretschmann (1991) conceptualizes solidarity as non-selfish, cooperative behavior and contrasts it in particular with behavior in the economic marketplace. As an orientation to social action, it stands for commitment and sacrifice on behalf of others. Among the participants in this form of network there are shared values, a shared view of the situation, and a consensus as to what events mean; clarity over norms is achieved through social approval and gossip, and hence the group's sense of propriety is revealed informally through talk (Kaufmann, 1991b).

Although this sort of network is situation-regarding, it may also take the form of an enclave or subgroup that is hostile or closed off to the broader society or new entrants.

In fact, it is the very informality of networks that gives rise to a certain hesitancy and concern about how they work and their impact. Coordination in this case may be settled in a less than open manner and not subject to any obvious accountability.

> A lot of networks are highly exclusive of outsiders. In one sense the Mafia is a
> perfect network structure. It relies upon informality, clan and kin loyalty; it is far
> from open; and has its own secret system of rewards and punishments which is
> quite clearly corrupt in many respects. (Frances, Levacic, Mitchell, & Thompson,
> 1991, p. 14)

We do not need to invoke the hyperbolic imagery of the Mafia or the hint
of corruption to appreciate that solidarity-based networks can be defined in
terms of provincial criteria. Another image that comes to mind is the roman-
ticized Irish community, complete with supralegal norm-enforcing networks
and stalwart, supportive associates. The critique of solidarity networks
corresponds to the critique of neotribalism presented in Chapter 3. Robust
subcultures are dialectically related to the "thin" macroculture, which fails
to unite the classes and factions of the English-speaking islands. But solidarity networks that can transcend the neotribalism, like some-talk discourse
that finds a way of including all relevant voices, do provide a hopeful image,
despite the disagreeable possibilities that are entailed with narrowly provincial subcultures.

A third danger of networks stems from the social pressures and norm-
creating interactions that are endemic to them.

3. Community Over All

This third sort of problem is glossed over by communitarians who, to their
credit we believe, argue for a stronger sense of the public thing, but lack a
good line of demarcation as to where the public thing should cease. Put
another way, we would like to retain a measure of libertarian tolerance for
those who step outside of the dominant social and moral codes. But Bellah,
Madsen, Sullivan, Swidler, and Tipton (1991) argue for a democratic society
that contains, among other things, a "public church." They are not intending
to prescribe a state religion or a governmental church, but, "in two senses,"
the authors of *The Good Society* write, "religion cannot be private."

> Firstly, both Christians and Jews recognize a God who created heaven and earth,
> all that is, seen and unseen, whose dominion clearly transcends not only private
> life but the nations themselves. There is nothing in the private or public realm that
> cannot concern such a religious tradition.
>   Secondly . . . "public" came to mean the citizenry who reflect on matters of
> common concern, engage in deliberation together, and choose their representatives
> to constitute the government, whose powers are limited by a constitution. Religious

bodies are very much part of *this* meaning of the public . . . because they enter into the common discussion about the public good. (Bellah et al., 1991, p. 179)

Bellah and his associates presume "religious bodies" are able to speak in the common discussion, a presumption that calls forth a series of problems lurking just beneath the surface of community.

a. Michels's Iron Law of Oligarchy

All the problems of few-talk—most particularly monologic manipulation—become problematic when organized hierarchies (of which Judaism and Christianity are but examples; the U.S. Chamber of Commerce or the United Auto Workers would be other private organizations that assert themselves forcefully in the public realm) enter the common discussion as if they were citizens. Michels (1915/1958) carefully argued that organization is necessary to the political struggle of the masses, because direct discussion does not lend itself to getting the work done. But the organization inclines toward oligarchy, and then the "aristocratic tendency" manifests itself. Democratic control undergoes a "progressive diminution," while discipline and subordination are elevated as values. The interests of the group/community begin to outweigh individual autonomy, which is muted by community leaders in the name of solidarity.

b. Reification of Institutions

One must first anthropomorphize a religious body before one can accept the notion that a reified abstraction such as religion or any other human structure (organization, corporation, family) can actually speak, as if it were a person having a discussion with others. In Chapter 4 we cited the work of Anthony Giddens (1984) on structuration to help us make the point that institutions (recursive practices) are embodied habits, traditions, and patterns of social interaction that present themselves as independent forces with their own being. But does this mean that entities can speak? The notion is preposterous when taken literally, because only people have larynxes and the necessary vocal musculature to carry out such a task. More to the point, the notion that some individual enters the discourse to speak "on behalf of" a social-structural contraption brings into question the authenticity of the speech act. The "on behalf of" speech acts that are welcome are those made on behalf of the public interest, but speech by an institution adopts a particularistic and narrow standpoint that is not primarily situation-regarding; it is, almost by definition, organization-regarding, which is to say particularistic. Positions are adopted and fully prescribed in accord with organizational imperatives, rather than the imperatives of the situation. Institutions ought not be allowed to, indeed do not, speak with the same authenticity that citizens do.[2]

c. Mistaking Entities for Citizens

Treating institutions like corporations as citizens has helped to solve public disputes that have cropped up before. In the 1837 Supreme Court case *Charles River Bridge v. Proprietors of Warren Bridge,* organizations (corporations, municipalities) were granted legal status equal to that of an individual citizen for most purposes. Although he lost the case defending a monopoly company against what the courts perceived as the public interest, Daniel Webster successfully argued on behalf of Charles River Bridge that corporations were to be considered "persons" with respect to the privileges and immunities clause in Article IV of the U.S. Constitution, which granted citizens of one state "the privileges and immunities of the citizens in the several states." The Supreme Court did not take it quite so far as to equate corporate entities with citizens, but almost.[3] Whatever the advantages of treating corporations as entities for purposes of economic dispute resolution, the practice does nothing to enhance the authenticity of the discourse. The speaker, if a corporation, is disembodied and therefore anonymous, and incapable of adopting a standpoint more abstract than self-interest. Whoever utters the corporate claims is necessarily a "mouth organ" and therefore suspect as a willing, attentive participant.

d. Intrusive Fussbudgets

Let us return now to the Bellah et al. (1991) quotation asserting that "There is nothing in the private or public realm that cannot concern such a religious tradition." Now if one is neither a Christian nor a Jew, the notion that Christians and Jews would declare the public at large (or "nations themselves") to be their domain is not necessarily reassuring. Indeed, with nothing off-limits to community strictures that are not one's own, one might be worried that one's opportunities to live life as one wishes in a non-Christian or non-Jewish manner would diminish. Private space is particularly vulnerable to communitarian encroachments. Stivers (1993) ridiculed an attempt to create a preserve of issues not subject to public deliberation.

Once during a meeting of public administration theorists I heard a well-known and respected figure say that he wanted a "structured public argument" that would

make certain questions "off limits"—an unusually frank and self-aware declara-
tion of a strategy by which intellectuals . . . achieve . . . a definitional or meta-
theoretical level of like-mindedness that keeps the world from being turned upside
down. But the insistence on maintaining these established boundaries . . . is at the
same time a strategy of legitimation *and* a strategy of suppression. (p. 126)

Stivers's point that keeping issues off the agenda is a form of domination is
well-taken. Certain kinds of personal issues—such as male domination of
females—must be politicized before the structural injustice in the way cultures
fashion these relationships can be debated. But consider another passage from
Stivers's book. She is speaking of the case of Oskar Schindler, known as a moral
hero for taking personal risk to save hundreds of Jews during World War II.
Stivers will not allow Schindler to have his moral heroism, as others, including
L. A. Blum (1988), who wrote *Moral Exemplars* (cited in Stivers, 1993), would
have allowed. Why? Because Schindler was a libertine (which the dictionary
defines as a freethinker on religious matters and/or one who is unrestrained by
conventional morality). Moreover, he impetuously practiced his libertinism by
taking two mistresses. So now the question for Stivers becomes, is Schindler
still a moral hero? Blum (quoted in Stivers, p. 93) considers the matter,
hedges, and then makes a judgment: Schindler is "less of a moral paragon than
he would otherwise be; but he remains, I think, a moral hero." Stivers (1993)
gives more weight to the importance of Schindler's erotic couplings:

Blum's assessment appears to be based on the assumption that sexual transgres-
sions—for example, the breaking of a trust between husband and wife—are less
important to a person's overall moral worth than willingness to risk one's life to
save the lives of others. (p. 93)

But, we argue, who wouldn't make such an assumption? Who would not
think saving Jews during the Holocaust to be the more substantial matter?
Stivers's rationale for questioning Schindler's heroism is presented as an
argument against the private realm/public realm dichotomy.

Part of my reluctance to discount Schindler's sexual behavior comes from a sense
that the dividing line between public and domestic realms has had the effect of
rendering men's domination and mistreatment of women relatively marginal to
the assessment of their characters. (Stivers, 1993, pp. 93-94)

Stivers has a good point. If domestic issues are not elevated, many issues
of concern to women will be left off the agenda. Yet, the more things called

sin, the more sin. There are some places where public administrators ought not tread, or at least ought to tread lightly, justly, rarely, and solicitously. We are unable to find the line where off-limits issues begin, but not all issues are public issues. The claims of pursed-lipped fussbudgets enforcing the lesser mandates of the community do not always trump the claims of the individual of classical liberalism.

The association here is that a coercively moral homogeneous community looks identical to a totalitarian state. We also described a community/ network that resembles the neotribe, after expressing misgivings about nondemocratic features of corporatist networks. By carefully explicating the nondemocratic and inauthentic aspects of policy networks, we have better identified the somewhat narrower range of authentic, democratic possibilities. The network formations we seek to avoid help shape what we aspire to: authentic discourse.

B. A PROACTIVE ROLE FOR PUBLIC ADMINISTRATION

The nondiscursive policy networks described above are, normatively, to be avoided in the quest for authentic discourse. But the nondiscourse potentialities will present themselves to practicing public administrators at least as frequently, we would assume, as do opportunities for authentic discourse. The burden of responsibilities for public administrators in sorting one from the other is formidable. Certainly life is more complicated for the public administrator who peeks out from the protective umbrella of neutral competence where technical criteria guided action. Expertise may well constitute a substantive contribution to the public discourse, but it must first be grounded in a public conversation about a situation. Politics is thus said to be an everyday activity for everyone involved in governance (Miller, 1993). The idea of government by discussion, of reaching public action through a process of agonistic discourse, drives the model of public administration advanced here. The permanent dispute in public policy discourse is not ultimately about what happened (explanation) or what will happen (prediction) although these questions matter; the dispute is over what should be done next. Resolving that question is not wholly a matter of applying known procedures, although procedural guidelines are often helpful. The matter is ultimately a question of ought, of wills, values, and persuasive capacity. Hence a proactive role for public administrators (Harmon, 1981) is inferred from the demands of the job.

1. Listening

Listening is a proactive responsibility implied by discourse theory. Failing to listen does damage. A nonlistening public administrator will be perceived as a bureaucratic drone, faithful only to "administrivia" (see Forester, 1989; see also Stivers, 1994)). Those who fail to listen miss information they would be better off knowing. Failing to listen means allowing the ideology of everyday life to go unchallenged (Forester, 1989). Becoming ideologically preoccupied with the abstractions of arguments can lead us to neglect the situation. Worse, nonlisteners lose membership in the common world of action where participants learn about the cares and fears of others, about common interests, about new arguments and strategies (Forester, 1989). Listening is work, but it also shows a caring attitude and expresses a desire for authentic discourse.

Listening also mitigates against self-delusion (Barber, 1984). Spoken words do not automatically express their meanings, which are contingent on the situation, which in turn implies context, history, or background events. Listeners can explore ambiguities whereas nonlisteners must presume more. The caring attitude that listening expresses also characterized the role of midwife (see Belenky, 1986).

Stivers (1993) credits Doug Morgan and Henry Kass for an intriguing image of public administrators as midwives: "The image of the midwife is of a skilled and caring person who facilitates the emergence of new possibilities" (p. 132). Hence the public administrator's role is to facilitate the discourse by getting disparate subgroups to speak the language of the public interest. And moreover, public administrators may themselves make substantive, even political contributions, but from an unelevated standpoint: "citizen *with* the rest of us" (Stivers, 1993).

If the public conversation is to be something other than a playground for the mightiest, there must be norms of discourse commonly understood and a community that shares a forum of interaction where viewpoints may confront one another. Arbitrary exclusion from the discourse (for lack of money, for example) should be replaced by a presumption of inclusion, which may be forfeited only upon instances of inauthentic speech acts.

Notes

1. It was unknown the extent to which their participation related to on-the-job duties. Sustained attention over a 2-year time span, we would offer as an hypothesis, is associated with work-related responsibilities.

2. This is why Harmon and Mayer (1986) disparage systems theory and Harmon (1981) chooses the face-to-face encounter as the basic unit of organization theory.

3. The legal status of the corporation was secured. Justice Roger B. Taney, writing for the majority, stated, "We think it is well settled that by the law of comity among nations, a corporation created by one sovereignty is permitted to make contracts in another, and to sue in its courts, and that the same law of comity prevails among the several sovereignties of this Union" (quoted in Janosik, 1987, p. 69). Hence the term *citizen* in Article III of the Constitution has been interpreted to mean that corporations, municipalities, and other organizations are deemed to be citizens, and corporations are endowed by their charters with legal existence as entities. (See *The Guide to American Law*, 1983, Vol. 2, p. 325, and Vol. 8, p. 132.) As a result of the case, it became clear that states could legislate against corporations for the sake of the public interest, a victory for the Jacksonian democrats, and, less noticed, *the right of corporations to do business in other states and to enjoy the protection of laws was firmly established.* The latter point is the more important one for our considerations, because the legal system now overtly recognized entities as citizens for most intents and purposes.

References

Adams, G. B., Bowerman, P. V., Dolbeare, K. M., & Stivers, C. (1990). Joining purpose to practice: A democratic identity for the public service. In H. D. Kass & B. Catron (Eds.), *Images and identities in public administration* (pp. 219-240). Newbury Park, CA: Sage.

Appleby, P. H. (1949). *Policy and administration.* University, AL: University of Alabama Press.

Arendt, H. (1963). *On revolution.* New York: Penguin.

Avineri, S. (1968). *The social and political thought of Karl Marx.* New York: Cambridge University Press.

Bachrach, P. (1967). *The theory of democratic elitism.* Boston: Little, Brown.

Ban, C., & Ingraham, P. (1984). Introduction. In P. Ingraham & C. Ban (Eds.), *Civil service reform: Legislating bureaucratic change* (pp. 1-10). Albany: State University of New York Press.

Barber, B. (1984). *Strong democracy: Participatory politics for a new age.* Berkeley: University of California Press.

Barnard, C. I. (1966). *The functions of the executive.* Cambridge, MA: Harvard University Press. (Original work published 1938)

Baudrillard, J. (1981). *For a critique of the political economy of the sign* (C. Levin, Trans.). St. Louis: Telos Press.

Baudrillard, J. (1983). *Simulations.* New York: Semiotext(e).

Beiner, R. (1983). *Political judgment.* Chicago: University of Chicago Press.

Belenky, M. F. (1986). *Women's ways of knowing: The development of self, voice, and mind.* New York: Basic Books.

Bellah, R. N., Madsen, R., Sullivan, W. M., Swidler, A., & Tipton, S. M. (1985). *Habits of the heart: Individualism and commitment in American life.* Berkeley: University of California Press.

Bellah, R. N., Madsen, R., Sullivan, W. M., Swidler, A., & Tipton, S. M. (1991). *The good society.* New York: Knopf.

Bellone, C. J., & Goerl, G. F. (1992). Reconciling public entrepreneurship and democracy. *Public Administration Review, 52*(2), 130-134.

Berger, P. L., & Luckmann, T. (1966). *The social construction of reality.* Garden City, NY: Doubleday.

Berlin, I. (1979). *Concepts and categories: Philosophical essays* (H. Hardy, Ed.). New York: Viking.

Bernstein, R. J. (1983). *Beyond objectivism and relativism: Science, hermeneutics, and praxis.* Philadelphia: University of Pennsylvania Press.

Bernstein, R. J. (1992). *The new constellation: The ethical-political horizons of modernity/post-modernity.* Cambridge: MIT Press.

Blum, L. A. (1988). Moral exemplars: Reflections on Schindler, the Trocmes, and others. *Midwest Studies in Philosophy, 12,* 135-150.

Blumenthal, S. (1980). *The permanent campaign.* Boston: Beacon Press.

Botwinick, A. (1993). *Postmodernism and democratic theory.* Philadelphia: Temple University Press.

Brudney, J. L., & England, R. E. (1982). Urban policy making and subjective service evaluations: Are they compatible? *Public Administration Review, 42,* 127-135.

Buchanan, J. H., & Tullock, G. (1962). *The calculus of consent: Logical foundations of constitutional democracy.* Ann Arbor: University of Michigan Press.

Burke, J. P. (1986). *Bureaucratic responsibility.* Baltimore: Johns Hopkins University Press.

Calhoun, C. (1992). Introduction: Habermas and the public sphere. In C. Calhoun (Ed.), *Habermas and the public sphere* (pp. 1-48). Cambridge MA: MIT Press.

Calinescu, M. (1991). From the one to the many: Pluralism in today's thought. In I. Hoesterey (Ed.), *Zeitgeist in Babel: The post-modernist controversy* (pp. 156-174). Bloomington: Indiana University Press.

Carnap, R. (1959a). The elimination of metaphysics through logical analysis of language (A. Pap, Trans.). In A. J. Ayer (Ed.), *Logical positivism* (pp. 60-81). New York: Free Press.

Carnap, R. (1959b). The old and the new logic (I. Levi, Trans.). In A. J. Ayer (Ed.), *Logical positivism* (pp. 133-146). New York: Free Press.

Chandler, R. C. (1984). The public administrator as representative citizen: A new role for the new century. *Public Administration Review, 44,* 196-206.

Clary, B. (1986, September). A framework for citizen participation: Portland's Office of Neighborhood Associations. *MIS Report, 18,* 1-13.

Coch, L., & French, J.R.P. (1948). Overcoming resistance to change. *Human Relations, 1,* 512-532.

Cochran, C. E. (1982). *Character, community and politics.* University, AL: University of Alabama Press.

Cooper, P. (1990). Appendix, selected responses. In G. L. Wamsley, R. N. Bacher, C. T. Goodsell, P. S. Kronenberg, J. A. Rohr, C. M. Stivers, O. F. White, & J. F. Wolf (Eds.), *Refounding public administration* (pp. 311-313). Newbury Park, CA: Sage.

Cooper, T. L. (1987). Hierarchy, virtue, and the practice of public administration: A perspective for normative ethics. *Public Administration Review, 47,* 320-328.

Cooper, T. L. (1991). *An ethic of citizenship for public administration.* Englewood Cliffs, NJ: Prentice Hall.

Crosby, N., Kelly, J. M., & Schaefer, P. (1986). Citizen panels: A new approach to citizen participation. *Public Administration Review, 52,* 170-178.

Dahl, R. (1971). *Polyarchy: Participation and opposition.* New Haven, CT: Yale University Press.

DeLeon, P. (1992). The democratization of the policy sciences. *Public Administration Review, 52*(2), 125-129.

d'Entreves, M. P. (1992). Communitarianism. In L. C. Becker (Ed.), *Encyclopedia of ethics* (Vol. 1, pp. 181-185). New York: Garland.

Dillman, D. L. (1984). Civil service reform in comparative perspective: The United States and Great Britain. In P. W. Ingraham & C. Ban (Eds.), *Legislating bureaucratic change: The Civil Service Reform Act of 1978* (pp. 203-217). Albany: State University of New York Press.

Duverger, M. (1955). *Political parties.* New York: John Wiley.

Edelman, M. (1964). *The symbolic uses of politics.* Urbana: University of Illinois Press.

Edelman, M. (1971). *Politics as symbolic action.* New York: Academic Press.
Edelman, M. (1977). *Political language: Words that succeed and policies that fail.* New York: Academic Press.
Edelman, M. (1988). *Constructing the political spectacle.* Chicago: University of Chicago Press.
Edie, J. M. (1967). Transcendental phenomenology and existentialism. In J. J. Kockelmans (Ed.), *Phenomenology.* Garden City, NY: Doubleday.
Edsall, T. B., & Edsall, M. D. (1991). *Chain reaction: The impact of race, rights and taxes on American politics.* New York: Norton.
Engel, J. F. (1968). *Consumer behavior.* Homewood, IL: Irwin.
Feuerbach, L. (1881). *The essence of Christianity* (M. Evans, Trans.). Boston: Houghton Mifflin.
Finer, H. (1936). Better government personnel. *Political Science Quarterly, 51,* 569-599.
Finer, H. (1941/1972). Administrative responsibility in democratic government. In F. Rourke (Ed.), *Bureaucratic power in national politics* (2nd ed.). Boston: Little, Brown.
Fischer, F. (1990). *Technocracy and the politics of expertise.* Newbury Park, CA: Sage.
Fitzgerald, M. R., & Durant, R. F. (1980). Citizen evaluations and urban management: Service delivery in an era of protest. *Public Administration Review, 40*(6), 585-594.
Follett, M. P. (1951). *Creative experience.* New York: Peter Smith. (Original work published 1924)
Follett, M. P. (1978). The giving of orders. In J. M. Shafritz & A. C. Hyde (Eds.), *Classics of public administration* (pp. 29-37). Oak Park, IL: Moore. (Original work published 1926)
Folz, D. H., & Hazlett, J. M. (1991). Public participation and recycling performance: Explaining program success. *Public Administration Review, 51*(6), 526-532.
Forester, J. (1989). *Planning in the face of power.* Berkeley: University of California Press.
Foucault, M. (1970). *The order of things.* New York: Pantheon.
Fox, C. J. (1980, September). The existential phenomenological alternative to dichotomous thought. *Western Political Quarterly, 33,* 357-379.
Fox, C. J. (1989). Free to choose, free to win, free to lose: The phenomenology of ethical space. *International Journal of Public Administration, 12*(6), 913-930.
Fox, C. J. (1990). Implementation research: Why and how to transcend positivist methodologies. In D. J. Palumbo & D. J. Calista (Eds.), *Implementation and the policy process: Opening up the black box* (pp. 199-212). New York: Greenwood.
Fox, C. J. (1991). Employee performance appraisal: The keystone made of clay. In C. Ban & N. M. Riccucci (Eds.), *Public personnel management: Current concerns—future challenges* (pp. 58-72). New York: Longman.
Fox, C. J. (1992). What do we mean when we say "professionalism"?: A language usage analysis for public administration. *American Review of Public Administration, 22*(1), 1-18.
Fox, C. J. (1993). The use of philosophy in public administration ethics. In T. Cooper (Ed.), *Handbook on administrative ethics* (pp. 83-106). New York: Marcel Dekker.
Fox, C. J., & Cochran, C. (1990). Discretionary public administration: Toward a Platonic guardian class? In H. D. Kass & B. Catron (Eds.), *Images and identities in public administration* (pp. 87-112). Newbury Park, CA: Sage.
Fox, C. J., & Miller, H. (1993). Postmodern public administration: A short treatise on self-referential epiphenomena. *Administration Theory and Praxis, 15*(1), 1-17.
Frances, J., Levacic, R., Mitchell, J., & Thompson, G. (1991). Introduction. In F. Thompson, R. Levacic, & J. Mitchell (Eds.), *Markets, hierarchies & networks: The coordination of social life.* Newbury Park, CA: Sage, and The Open University.
Fraser, N. (1992). Rethinking the public sphere: A contribution to the critique of actually existing democracy. In C. Calhoun (Ed.), *Habermas and the public sphere.* Cambridge: MIT Press.
Fredrickson, H. G. (1982). The recovery of civism in public administration. *Public Administration Review, 42,* 501-508.

Gawthrop, L. C. (1984). Civis, civitas and civilitas: A new focus for the year 2000. *Public Administration Review, 34,* 101-107.

Giddens, A. (1984). *The constitution of society: Outline of the theory of structuration.* Berkeley: University of California Press.

Giddens, A. (1990). *The consequences of modernity.* Stanford, CA: Stanford University Press.

Goodsell, C. (1990). Public administration and the public interest. In G. L. Wamsley, R. N. Bacher, C. T. Goodsell, P. S. Kronenberg, J. A. Rohr, C. M. Stivers, O. F. White, & J. F. Wolf (Eds.), *Refounding public administration* (pp. 96-113). Newbury Park, CA: Sage.

Goodsell, C. T. (1994). *The case for bureaucracy* (3rd ed.). Chatham, NJ: Chatham House.

Gore, A. (1993). *Report of the national performance review: From red tape to results: Creating a government that works better and costs less.* Washington, DC: U.S. Government Printing Office.

Granovetter, M. (1985). Economic action and social structure: The problem of embeddedness. *American Journal of Sociology, 91*(3), 481-510.

Gretschmann, K. (1991). Solidarity and markets reconsidered: Cum, versus, or what? In F. Kaufmann (Ed.), *The public sector: Challenge for coordination and learning* (pp. 395-415). Berlin: Walter de Gruyter.

Grodzins, M. (1966). *The American system: A new view of government in the United States.* Chicago: Rand McNally.

Guba, E. (1985). The context of emergent paradigm research. In Y. S. Lincoln (Ed.), *Organizational theory and inquiry: The paradigm revolution* (pp. 79-104). Beverly Hills, CA: Sage.

Habermas, J. (1972). *Knowledge and human interests* (J. J. Shapiro, Trans.). Boston: Beacon Press.

Habermas, J. (1975). *Legitimation crisis* (T. McCarthy, Trans.). Boston: Beacon Press.

Habermas, J. (1989). *The structural transformation of the public sphere* (T. Burger & F. Lawrence, Trans.). Cambridge: MIT Press.

Habermas, J. (1992). In C. Calhoun (Ed.), *Habermas and the public sphere.* (pp. 421-461). Cambridge: MIT Press.

Hall, J. S., & Weschler, L. F. (1991). The Phoenix Futures Forum: Creating vision, implanting community. *National Civic Review, 80*(Spring), 135-157.

Halpin, J. F. (1966). *Zero defects: A new dimension in quality assurance.* New York: McGraw-Hill.

Harmon, M. M. (1981). *Action theory for public administration.* New York: Longman.

Harmon, M. M., & Mayer, R. T. (1986). *Organization theory for public administration.* Boston: Little Brown.

Hawking, S. W. (1988). *A brief history of time.* New York: Bantam.

Heclo, H. (1978). Issue networks and the executive establishment. In A. King (Ed.), *The new American political system* (pp. 87-124). Washington, DC: American Enterprise Institute for Public Policy Research.

Hines, B. (1986, April). Health policy on the town meeting agenda. *Hastings Center Report,* pp. 5-7.

Hirsh, A. (1981). *The French new left: An intellectual history from Sartre to Gorz.* Boston: South End Press.

Honig, B. (1992). Toward an agonistic feminism: Hannah Arendt and the politics of identity. In J. Butler & J. W. Scott (Eds.), *Feminists theorize the political.* New York: Routledge.

Hummel, R. P. (1994). *The bureaucratic experience: A critique of life in the modern organization.* New York: St. Martin's Press.

Husserl, E. (1962). *Ideas: General introduction to pure phenomenology.* London: Collier.

Huxtable, A. L. (1992, December 3). Inventing American reality. *New York Review of Books, 39*(20), 24-29.

Ingersoll, V. H., & Adams, G. B. (1992). *The tacit organization.* Greenwich, CT: JAI Press.

Jahn, R. G., & Dunne, B. J. (1986). On the quantum mechanics of consciousness, with application to anomalous phenomena. *Foundations of Physics, 16*(8), 721-772.

Jameson, F. (1991). *Postmodernism or the cultural logic of late capitalism.* Durham, NC: Duke University Press.

Jammer, M. (1967). Energy. In P. Edwards (Ed.), *The encyclopedia of philosophy* (Vol. 2, pp. 511-517). New York: Macmillan.

Jamieson, K. H. (1992). *Dirty politics: Deception, distraction and democracy.* New York: Oxford University Press.

Janosik, R. J. (1987). *Encyclopedia of the American judicial system: Studies of the principal institutions and processes of law.* New York: Scribner's.

Jencks, C. (1991). Postmodern vs. late-modern. In I. Hoesterey (Ed.). *Zeitgeist in Babel: The post-modernist controversy* (pp. 4-21). Bloomington: Indiana University Press.

Jonsen, A. R., & Toulmin, S. (1988). *The abuse of casuistry: A history of moral reasoning.* Berkeley: University of California Press.

Kathlene, L., & Martin, J. A. (1991). Enhancing citizen participation: Panel designs, perspectives, and policy formulation. *Journal of Policy Analysis and Management, 10*(1), 46-63.

Kaufmann, F. (1991a). Introduction: Issues and context. In F. Kaufmann (Ed.), *The public sector: Challenge for coordination and learning* (pp. 3-28). Berlin: Walter de Gruyter.

Kaufmann, F. (1991b). The relationship between guidance, control, and evaluation. In F. Kaufmann (Ed.), *The public sector: Challenge for coordination and learning* (pp. 213-234). Berlin: Walter de Gruyter.

Keller, L. F. (1984). The political economy of public management: An interorganizational network perspective. *Administration and Society, 15,* 455-474.

Kellner, D. (1989). *Jean Baudrillard: From Marxism to postmodernism and beyond.* Stanford, CA: Stanford University Press.

Kellner, D. (1990). *Television and the crisis of democracy.* Boulder, CO: Westview Press.

Kingdon, J. W. (1984). *Agendas, alternatives, and public policies.* Boston: Little, Brown.

Knott, J. H., & Miller, G. J. (1987). *Reforming bureaucracy: The politics of institutional choice.* Englewood Cliffs, NJ: Prentice Hall.

Kockelmans, J. J. (Ed.). (1967). *Phenomenology: The philosophy of Edmund Husserl and its interpretation.* Garden City, NY: Doubleday.

Kronenberg, P. S. (1990). Public administration and the Defense Department: Examination of a prototype. In G. L. Wamsley, R. N. Bacher, C. T. Goodsell, P. S. Kronenberg, J. A. Rohr, C. M. Stivers, O. F. White, & J. F. Wolf (Eds.), *Refounding public administration* (pp. 274-306). Newbury Park, CA: Sage.

Kuhn, T. (1970). *The structure of scientific revolutions* (2nd ed.). Chicago: University of Chicago Press.

Kwant, R. C. (1963). *Phenomenological philosophy of Merleau-Ponty.* Pittsburgh: Duquesne University Press.

Langan, T. (1966). *Merleau-Ponty's critique of reason.* New Haven, CT: Yale University Press.

Levine, A., & Silverstein, K. (1993, December 13). How the drug lobby cut cost controls. *Nation,* pp. 1ff.

Lewin, K. (1951). *Field theory in social science.* In D. Cartwright, (Ed.). New York: Harper.

Lindblom, C. E. (1977). *Politics and markets: The world's political-economic systems.* New York: Basic Books.

Lipsky, M. (1980). *Street-level bureaucracy: Dilemmas of the individual in public services.* New York: Russell Sage.

Lloyd, G.E.R. (1967). Leucippus and Democritus. In P. Edwards (Ed.), *The encyclopedia of philosophy* (Vol. 3, pp. 446-451). New York: Macmillan.

Lowi, T. J. (1969). *The end of liberalism: Ideology, policy, and the crisis of public authority.* New York: W. W. Norton.

Lowi, T. J. (1979). *The end of liberalism: The second republic of the United States.* New York: W. W. Norton.

Lowi, T. J. (1993). Legitimizing public administration: A disturbed dissent. *Public Administration Review, 53*(3), 261-264.

Lyotard, J.-F. (1984). *The postmodern condition: A report on knowledge* (G. Bennington & B. Massumi, Trans.) Minneapolis: University of Minnesota Press.

MacIntyre, A. (1981). *After virtue.* Notre Dame, IN: Notre Dame University Press.

MacIntyre, A. (1984). *After virtue* (2nd ed.). Notre Dame, IN: Notre Dame University Press.

Mallin, S. (1979) *Merleau-Ponty's philosophy.* New Haven: Yale University Press.

Marcuse, H. (1964). *One dimensional man: Studies in the ideology of advanced industrial society.* Boston: Beacon Press.

McCarthy, T. (1975). Translator's Preface. In J. Habermas, *Legitimation crisis* (pp. i-xxiv). Boston: Beacon Press.

Merleau-Ponty, M. (1962). *The phenomenology of perception* (C. Smith, Trans.). New York: Humanities Press.

Merleau-Ponty, M. (1963). *The structure of behavior.* A. L. Fisher (Trans.). Boston: Beacon Press.

Mertins, H., & Hennigan, P. J. (1982). *Applying professional standards and ethics in the eighties: A workbook and study guide for public administrators.* Washington, DC: American Society for Public Administration.

Merton, R. (1957). *Social theory and social structure.* Glencoe, IL: Free Press.

Michels, R. (1958). *Political parties: A sociological study of the oligarchical tendencies of modern democracy.* Glencoe, IL: Free Press. (Original work published 1915)

Miller, H. T. (1993). Everyday politics in public administration. *American Review of Public Administration, 23*(2), 99-116.

Miller, H. T. (1994). Postprogressive public administration: Lessons from policy networks. *Public Administration Review, 54*(4), 378-385.

Moore, S. (1987). *Street-level tasks: A decision making approach.* Paper presented at Annual Meeting of American Political Science Association, Chicago.

Morgan, D. F. (1990). Administrative phronesis: Discretion and the problem of administrative legitimacy in our constitutional system. In H. D. Kass & B. Catron (Eds.), *Images and identities in public administration* (pp. 67-86). Newbury Park, CA: Sage.

Morgan, G. (1986). *Images of organization.* Newbury Park, CA: Sage.

Mosher, F. C. (1982). *Democracy and the public service* (2nd ed.). New York: Oxford University Press.

Nachmias, D., & Nachmias, C. (1988). *Research methods in the social sciences* (3rd ed.). New York: St. Martin's.

Neurath, O. (1959). Protocol sentences (G. Schick, Trans.). In A. J. Ayer (Ed.), *Logical positivism* (pp. 199-208). New York: Free Press.

Oakeshott, M. (1991). *Rationalism in politics and other essays.* Indianapolis: Liberty Press.

Ollman, B. (1971). *Alienation: Marx's conception of man in capitalist society.* Cambridge: Cambridge University Press.

Ott, J. S. (1989). *The organizational culture perspective.* Pacific Grove, CA: Brooks/Cole.

Overman, E. S. (1991). Policy physics. In T. L. Becker (Ed.), *Quantum politics: Applying quantum theory to political phenomena* (pp. 151-167). New York: Praeger.

Page, B., & Brody, R. (1972). Policy voting and the electoral process. *American Political Science Review, 66,* 979-995.

Parenti, M. (1983). *Democracy for the few* (4th ed.). New York: St. Martin's Press.

Pateman, C. (1970). *Participation and democratic theory.* London: Cambridge University Press.

Pfeffer, J. (1981). *Power in organizations.* Boston: Pittman.

Plant, J. F. (1983). Ethics and public personnel administration. In S. W. Hays & R. C. Kearney (Eds.), *Public personnel administration* (pp. 289-308). Englewood Cliffs, NJ: Prentice Hall.

Poster, M. (1989). *Critical theory and poststructuralism: In search of a context.* Ithaca, NY: Cornell University Press.

Poster, M. (1990). *The mode of information: Poststructuralism and social context.* Chicago: University of Chicago Press.

Powell, W. W. (1990). Neither market nor hierarchy: Network forms of organization. *Research in Organizational Behavior, 12,* 295-336.

Prewitt, K. (1970). Political ambitions, volunteerism, and electoral accountability. *American Political Science Review, 64,* 5-17.

Roethlisberger, F. J., & Dickson, W. J. (1939). *Management and the worker.* Cambridge, MA: Harvard University Press.

Rohr, J. A. (1986). *To run a constitution: The legitimacy of the administrative state.* Lawrence: University Press of Kansas.

Rohr, J. A. (1989). *Ethics for bureaucrats: An essay on law and values* (2nd ed.). New York: Marcel Dekker.

Rohr, J. A. (1993). Toward a more perfect union. *Public Administration Review, 53*(3), 246-249.

Rorty, R. (1979). *Philosophy and the mirror of nature.* Princeton, NJ: Princeton University Press.

Russell, L. J. (1967). Leibniz, Gottfried Wilhelm. In P. Edwards (Ed.), *The encyclopedia of philosophy* (Vol. 3, pp. 422-435). New York: Macmillan.

Sanford, T. (1967). *Storm over the states.* New York: McGraw-Hill.

Schattschneider, E. E. (1960). *The semisovereign people: A realist's view of democracy in America.* New York: Holt, Rinehart & Winston.

Schon, D. A. (1971). *Beyond the stable state: Public and private learning in a changing society.* London: Temple Smith.

Simonsen, B., Collins, N., & Barnett, R. (1993, April). *Attempting non-incremental budget change in Oregon: An exercise in policy sharing.* Paper presented at Western Social Sciences Association, Corpus Christi, Texas.

Smith, M. J. (1991). From policy communication to issue networks: Salmonella in eggs and the new politics of food. *Public Administration, 69*(Summer), 234-255.

Spicer, M. W., & Terry, L. D. (1993). Legitimacy, history, and logic: Public administration and the Constitution. *Public Administration Review, 53*(3), 239-246.

Steinfels, P. (1979). *Neoconservatives: The men who are changing America's politics.* New York: Simon & Schuster.

Stewart, T. R., Dennis, R. L., & Ely, D. W. (1984). Citizen participation and judgment in policy analysis: A case study of urban air quality policy. *Policy Sciences, 17*(May), 67-87.

Stipak, B. (1980). Local governments' use of citizen surveys. *Public Administration Review, 40*(5), 521-525.

Stivers, C. M. (1990a). Active citizenship and public administration. In G. L. Wamsley, R. N. Bacher, C. T. Goodsell, P. S. Kronenberg, J. A. Rohr, C. M. Stivers, O. F. White, & J. F. Wolf (Eds.), *Refounding public administration* (pp. 246-273). Newbury Park, CA: Sage.

Stivers, C. (1990b). The public agency as polis: Active citizenship in the administrative state. *Administration & Society, 22*(1), 86-105.

Stivers, C. (1993). *Gender images in public administration: Legitimacy and the administrative state.* Newbury Park, CA: Sage.

Stivers, C. (1994). The listening bureaucrat: Responsiveness in public administration. *Public Administration Review, 54*(4), 364-369.

Stone, D. A. (1988). *Policy paradox and political reason.* Glenview, IL: Scott Foresman/Little, Brown.

Suleiman, S. R. (1991). Feminism and postmodernism: A question of politics. In I. Hoesterey (Ed.), *Zeitgeist in Babel: The post-modernist controversy* (pp. 111-131). Bloomington: Indiana University Press.

Sundquist, J. L. (1973). *Dynamics of the party system: Alignment and realignment of political parties in the United States.* Washington DC: Brookings.

Taylor, C. (1985). *Philosophical papers* (2 vols.). Cambridge, MA: Cambridge University Press.

Taylor, F. W. (1978). Testimony before the U.S. House of Representatives, January 25. In J. M. Shafritz & A. C. Hyde (Eds.), *Classics of public administration.* Oak Park, IL: Moore. (Original work published 1912)

Thayer, F. C. (1978). The president's management "reforms": Theory X triumphant. *Public Administration Review, 38*(4), 309-314.

Thomas, J. M. (1985). Neighborhood response to redevelopment in Detroit. *Community Development Journal, 20*(7), 89-98.

U.S. Office of Personnel Management. (1979). Common themes in public personnel reform. *Personnel Management Reform, 1*(1), 1-7.

U.S. Senate, Committee on Government Affairs. (1978). Hearings on S. 2604, S. 2707, and S. 2830, Appendix, 95th Congress., 2d Sess. Washington, DC: Author.

Villa, D. R. (1992). Postmodernism and the public sphere. *American Political Science Review, 86*(3), 712-721.

Waldo, D. (1948). *The administrative state: A study of the political theory of American public administration.* New York: Ronald Press.

Wallace, B. A. (1989). *Choosing reality: A contemplative view of physics and the mind.* Boston: New Science Library.

Walton, M. (1986). *The Deming management method.* New York: Perrigg.

Walzer, M. (1970). *Obligations: Essays on disobedience, war, and citizenship.* Cambridge, MA: Harvard University Press.

Walzer, M. (1983). *Spheres of justice.* New York: Basic Books.

Wamsley, G. L. (1985). Policy subsystems as a unit of analysis in implementation studies: A struggle for theoretical synthesis. In K. Hanf & T.A.J. Toonen (Eds.), *Policy implementation in federal and unitary systems: Questions of analysis and design* (pp. 71-96). Dordrecht, Boston: Martinus Nijhoff.

Wamsley, G. L. (1990). Introduction. In G. L. Wamsley, R. N. Bacher, C. T. Goodsell, P. S. Kronenberg, J. A. Rohr, C. M. Stivers, O. F. White, & J. F. Wolf (Eds.), *Refounding public administration* (pp. 19-29). Newbury Park, CA: Sage.

Wamsley, G. L., Bacher, R. N., Goodsell, C. T., Kronenberg, P. S., Rohr, J. A., Stivers, C. M., White, O. F. & Wolf, J. F. (Eds.). (1990). *Refounding public administration.* Newbury Park, CA: Sage.

Watson, D. J., Juster, R. J., & Johnson, G. W. (1991). Institutionalized use of citizen surveys in the budgetary and policy-making processes: A small city case study. *Public Administration Review, 51*(3), 232-239.

Weber, M. (1946). *From Max Weber: Essays in sociology* (H. H. Gerth & C. W. Mills, Eds. and Trans.). New York: Oxford University Press.

Whiteside, K. H. (1988). *Merleau-Ponty and the foundation of an existential politics.* Princeton, NJ: Princeton University Press.

Williamson, O. E. (1975). *Markets and hierarchies: Analysis and antitrust implications—A study in the economics of internal organization.* New York: Free Press.

Wittgenstein, L. (1953). *Philosophical investigations.* New York: Macmillan.

Wolff, R. P., Moore, B., & Marcuse, H. (1965). *A critique of pure tolerance.* Boston: Beacon Press.

Yankelovich, D. (1991). *Coming to public judgment: Making democracy work in a complex world.* Syracuse, NY: Syracuse University Press.

Name Index

Subject Index

About the Authors

Charles J. Fox is a Professor of Political Science and Director of the Center for Public Service at Texas Tech University. He presides over a NASPAA-accredited program for Master of Public Administration that emphasizes municipal government and city management. He received his B.A. from the University of California, Santa Barbara, in intellectual history. His Ph.D. in government is from the Claremont Graduate School. He writes and teaches in the areas of public policy implementation, public personnel administration, ethics and administration, and public administration theory. His work has appeared in *Western Political Quarterly, Public Policy Review, Administration and Society, American Review of Public Administration, Public Personnel Review, International Journal of Public Administration,* and *Administrative Theory & Praxis.* He has also contributed to many anthologies. He was originally trained in political philosophy, but his primary focus over the last 10 years has been in public administration/policy. His intellectual project has been to do applied political philosophy: to bring traditional and especially contemporary philosophical scholarship to bear on the problematics of American governance.

Hugh T. Miller is Associate Professor and teaches "Political and Social Theories of Public Administration" (among other courses) in the M.P.A. Program at the University of Wisconsin, Oshkosh. He serves as coordinator of that program. He earned his Ph.D. from the American University in Washington, D.C., where his fields included organization development, quantitative methods of policy analysis, and governmental management. He earned an M.P.A. degree, also from American University, and a B.A. from Michigan State University in a multidisciplinary social science program. His scholarly work has appeared in *Public Administration Review, American Review of Public Administration, Policy Studies Journal, Public Productivity and Management Review, PS: Political Science and Politics,* and *Administrative Theory & Praxis.* His scholarly attention is persistently drawn to the paradoxes found at the intersection of democracy and administration.